Sylvia Wheeldon
Colin Campbell
Christina de la Mare
Airton Pozo de Mattos

Achieve 2
2nd edition
Student Book

OXFORD
UNIVERSITY PRESS

OXFORD
UNIVERSITY PRESS

Great Clarendon Street, Oxford, OX2 6DP, United Kingdom

Oxford University Press is a department of the University of Oxford. It furthers the University's objective of excellence in research, scholarship, and education by publishing worldwide. Oxford is a registered trade mark of Oxford University Press in the UK and in certain other countries

© Oxford University Press 2014

The moral rights of the author have been asserted

First published in 2014

2018 2017 2016

10 9 8 7 6

No unauthorized photocopying

All rights reserved. No part of this publication may be reproduced, stored in a retrieval system, or transmitted, in any form or by any means, without the prior permission in writing of Oxford University Press, or as expressly permitted by law, by licence or under terms agreed with the appropriate reprographics rights organization. Enquiries concerning reproduction outside the scope of the above should be sent to the ELT Rights Department, Oxford University Press, at the address above

You must not circulate this work in any other form and you must impose this same condition on any acquirer

Links to third party websites are provided by Oxford in good faith and for information only. Oxford disclaims any responsibility for the materials contained in any third party website referenced in this work

ISBN: 978 0 19 455641 5

Printed in China

This book is printed on paper from certified and well-managed sources

ACKNOWLEDGEMENTS

Alamy Images pp.7 (Party/blickwinkel), 10 (modern lounge/Victor Zastolskiy), 10 (traditional lounge/Chris Rose/PropertyStock), 14 (drilling rig/Leo Francini), 32 (flats/Pat Tuson), 32 (Amish carriage/Jeff Greenberg), 32 (wood/Inan Avci), 34 (girl with phone/Chris Rout), 36 (Amish women/brt COMM), 48 (Vegetable garden/Derek Harris), 52 (Juvenile detention centre/ZUMA Wire Service), 55 (teenage argument/Richard Newton), 86 (tourists/Ozimages), 88 (Jeroen Koolhaas & Dre Urhahn/AlamyCelebrity), 88 (Favelas, Brazil/Alamy Celebrity), 112 (ant/Papilio), 115 (Aboriginal boy/Deco), 123 (girl on laptop/Robin Beckham/BEEPstock), 128 (tractor sign/Patti McConville), 130 (American justice/Joe Belanger); Casulo p.13 (Casulo product assembly photos/Marcel Krings); Corbis pp.4 (teen girl/Wavebreak Media Ltd.), 28 (music students/Hill Street Studios/Blend Images), 30 (recording studio/Datacraft Co. Ltd), 37 (dog sled/Arctic-Images), 93 (young architect/Mika/Comet), 108 (One Direction/John A. Angelillo), 109 (Beatriz Milhazes/Georgios Kefalas/EPA), 112 (native man/Herve Collart/Sygma), 112 (coming-of-age ceremony/Jianan Yu/Reuters), 122 (Vintage TV/John Smith), 124 (rice power/Subhash Sharma/Zuma Press), 129 (Emperor penguin & chicks/Frans Lanting), cover (Violin on sheet music/Chris Stock/Lebrecht Music & Arts), cover (Computer monitor with graphs/Saul Gravy/Ikon Images), cover (Apple iPad/Ramin Talaie), cover (Man reading/Tomas Rodriguez); Getty Images pp.4 (college student/Jacqueline Veissid/Photodisc), 4 (teen girl/Ron Levine/Lifesize), 4 (smiling boy/Ryan McVay), 12 (man with laundry/Bruce Laurance/Photographer's Choice), 14 (cotton picker/John Philips/Time & Life Pictures), 14 (stadium construction/Adenilson Nunes/LatinContent), 16 (fruit picker/Isabelle Plasschaert/Photolibrary), 20 (women's football/Scott Heavey), 20 (Marta Vieira da Silva/Stuart Franklin/FIFA), 22 (Gilberto Godoy Filho/Damien Meyer/AFP), 24 (Man swimming underwater/Koji Aoki), 31 (Rihanna/Mike Coppola), 32 (Amish family/Martin Rogers/Stone), 40 (teen couple/Bellurget Jean Louis/StockImage), 50 (sulky teen girl/Susanne Walstrom/Johner Images), 88 (Favela painting, Rio De Janeiro/Fred Alves/Barcroft Media), 90 (glass apartments/Barry Winiker/Photolibrary), 91 (heavy snowfall/George White Location Photography/Photolibrary), 96 (library/Nancy Honey/Taxi), 100 (Tokyo marathon/Sankei), 102 (Australian Olympics athletes/Matt King), 103 (goalkeeper & cat/Andrew Powell/Liverpool FC), 104 (worried traveller/ColorBlind Images/Iconica), 105 (Henry Cejudo/G Newman Lowrance), 108 (Nicky Minaj/Jason LaVeris/FilmMagic), 112 (Quinceanera/Erin Patrice O'Brien/Taxi), 114 (Professor Dan Everett/Jose More/Chicago Tribune/MCT), 117 (Dayak Tribe Festival/Barry Kusuma/Photolibrary), 134 (reporter/DreamPictures/Photographer's Choice); iStockphoto pp.20 (sport icons/Marina Zlochin), 38 (culture icons/Brandon Laufenberg), 50 (Newspapers/Sherwin McGehee), 50 (bamboo texture/Sunnybeach), 84 (love icons/Helle Bro Clemmernsen), 87 (cinema/Denis Raev), 132 (counselling/Carmen Martinez Banus); Jordan Passman p.106 (Jordan Passman); Masterfile p.50 (father & son); Oxford University Press pp.14 (woman/Radius Images), 16 (girl on phone/amana images Inc.), 19 (celebrity/image100), 20 (Glass surface), 20 (football/Photodisc), 49 (electric car/Cultura); Press Association Images p.130 (Judge Michael Cicconetti/Tony Dejak/AP); Rex Features pp.4 (teen girl/Monkey Business Images), 38 (Big Brother logo), 38 (Big Brother 9 group/Channel 4), 43 ('I Love Lucy'/Everett Collection), 46 (New York Restoration Project/Startraks Photo), 110 (Coldplay/Brian Rasic), 111 (Emeli Sande/Steve Meddle), 120 (New Girl 2012/Twentieth Century Fox/Everett); Richard Aitken p.26 (Ruth Royall); Robert Harding World Imagery p.116 (coastal scene/Ken Gillham); Ryan Siu Motion + Pictures p.106 (Anthony Volodkin/Ryan Siu); SuperStock pp.5 (couple at fair/Fancy), 6 (Paris/MIVA Stock), 12 (woman on phone/OJO Images), 16 (coffee shop assistant/Tetra Images), 28 (playing guitar/Blend Images), 41 (make-up/fStop), 85 (couple/Image Source), 92 (lifeguard hut/Richard Cummins), 94 (exercising/Westend61), 99 (shaking hands/Tetra Images), 121 (dentist/Flirt), 133 (stolen bike/Image Source); Survival International p.116 (Boa Sr/© Anvita Abbi/Survival International).

Illustrations by: Estudio Albertoyos pp.107, 131; Martin Sanders/Beehive Illustration pp.44 (map), 118; Norbert Sipos/Beehive Illustration p.9.

Contents

STUDENT BOOK	Reading	Vocabulary	Grammar
Starter unit p4 Relationships	**Relationships** *Magazine article about how people's relationships began*	**Language workshop** • *do* and *make* • Phrasal verbs: relationships	**Tense review** Present and past tenses Future forms
Unit 1 p8 Home Sweet Home	**TinyDwelling** *Brochure about the small living movement* • **Strategy:** using previous knowledge	**Adjectives: home and place** **Language workshop** • *so … that / such … that* • Conjunctions of purpose	**Present perfect simple and continuous**
Unit 2 p14 The World of Work	**The Brazilian Dream** *Magazine article about economic migration to Brazil* • **Strategy:** multiple choice questions	**Adjectives: personal qualities** **Language workshop** • Negative prefixes • Easily-confused words	**Modals**
Unit 3 p20 Sports Heroes	**Pele in a skirt** *Profile of soccer player Marta* • **Strategy:** answering in your own words	**Adjectives: physical attributes** **Language workshop** • *too / not … enough* • Noun suffixes (1)	**Past perfect**
Unit 4 p26 A Career in Music	**Heading for stardom** *Review of a musical performer* • **Strategy:** understanding pronouns	**Verbs: music** **Language workshop** • Gerunds and infinitives (1) • Noun suffixes (2)	**Relative clauses (1)**
Unit 5 p32 Different Worlds	**A period of freedom** *Magazine article about Amish teenagers* • **Strategy:** using paragraph subheadings	**Verbs: lifestyle choices** **Language workshop** • Gerunds and infinitives (2) • Prefixes	**Relative clauses (2)**
Unit 6 p38 TV Trends	**Is reality TV worth watching?** *Opinion essay about reality TV* • **Strategy:** making inferences	**Television** **Language workshop** • *-ed* and *-ing* adjectives • *have / get something done*	**The passive (1)**
Unit 7 p44 Protecting Our Planet	**Transition to a world without oil** *Infographic about the Transition Movement* • **Strategy:** identifying synonyms and antonyms	**Verbs: environment** **Language workshop** • *either … or / neither … nor* • Prefixes and suffixes	**The passive (2)**
Unit 8 p50 Bad Behavior	**A new approach to youth crime** *News article about a new treatment for young offenders* • **Strategy:** using the context	**Verbs: crime and criminals** **Language workshop** • Reporting verbs • Expressions of time and place	**Reported speech**

Language reference
• Essentials p56 • Irregular verbs p59 • False friends p60 • Unit summaries p62 • Word list p80

Workbook p83

Starter

Relationships
Reading

Stage 1 Get ready!

1 Read the *Reading strategy* and the magazine article. Follow steps 1–3. Which is the most appropriate title?

A The perfect relationship
B Tips for a successful first date
C How my relationship began

Reading strategy

Choosing a title for a text
1 Skim the text to understand the main idea.
2 Decide which title is the best match for the text.
3 Read the text again quickly to check your answer.

Stage 2 Read and understand

2 🔊 1.02 Read the article again. Complete the sentences with the correct names from the article.

1 _____ chose nicer clothes than _____ for their date.
2 _____ didn't arrive for his first date with _____.
3 _____ met _____ while he was visiting her country.
4 _____ and _____ met through a friend.
5 _____ noticed when _____ arrived.

3 According to the article, are the statements true (*T*) or false (*F*)?

1 Maria didn't mind that Brad was wearing old clothes. ____
2 Jorge thinks Isabel is good-looking. ____
3 Claudia didn't want to meet James. ____
4 Kakeru and Noriko went to the theater for their date. ____
5 Jens is going to see Beatriz in Portugal soon. ____

Maria: I always used to make an effort before a first date because I think that first impressions are important. I did my hair and wore a new dress. Brad wore old jeans and a T-shirt with a hole in it. But it didn't make any difference. I fell for him right away!

Jorge: The first time I saw Isabel she really made an impression on me. I was talking to friends at a party when suddenly this gorgeous girl walked in. I decided to ask for her phone number. Two years later, we're still going out!

Claudia: Last week I made plans to meet James for a coffee. It was our first date and I was looking forward to it, but he let me down! Was I upset? A little, but I got over it. We arranged another date and he arrived on time!

Kakeru: My friend Riku really did me a favor when he introduced me to his friend Noriko. She was so cute and we were interested in the same things. I asked her out and we went to see a movie. We're going to the same college this fall. I don't think we'll ever break up.

Beatriz: Jens and I met on a beach near my home in Faro, Portugal. He lives in Germany, but he was on vacation here. A long-distance relationship is hard work, but we do our best to keep in touch with texts and Skype. I'm going to visit him in Germany soon. I can't wait!

Vocabulary

Relationships

do and make

- We form a lot of collocations with *do* or *make*.
  – We **do our best**.
  – I **made plans** to meet James.

Language reference page 63

1 Write *do* or *make* to complete the collocations below.

1 _____ a / any difference
2 _____ someone a favor
3 _____ well
4 _____ an impression
5 _____ (your) best
6 _____ friends
7 _____ (your) hair
8 _____ an effort

2 Complete the sentences with the collocations in exercise 1. Use the correct form of *do* or *make*.

1 Wow! A pink and orange dress? You're going to _____!
2 The traffic is bad, but I'll _____ my _____ to be there as soon as possible.
3 Jack _____ at school. He gets straight As in all his subjects.
4 I took some medicine, but it didn't _____. I still felt terrible.
5 Ana is very sociable. She finds it easy to _____.
6 Can you _____ me _____? Is it OK if I borrow your laptop?

Phrasal verbs: relationships

- Phrasal verbs normally have two parts: a verb, and a preposition or adverb.
- Some phrasal verbs are separable. We must put the pronoun between the two parts.
  – I **asked** her **out**. ✓
  – I asked out her. ✗

Language reference page 63

3 Find the phrasal verbs below in the magazine article on page 4. Circle the correct meanings.

1 go out
  A go on a date
  B have a romantic relationship with someone
2 break up
  A end a relationship with someone
  B do someone physical harm
3 let down
  A not allow someone to do what they want
  B fail to meet or support someone as expected
4 ask out
  A ask someone for their personal information
  B invite someone on a date
5 fall for
  A not like someone
  B feel suddenly in love with someone
6 get over
  A stop feeling sad about something or someone
  B have a good relationship with someone

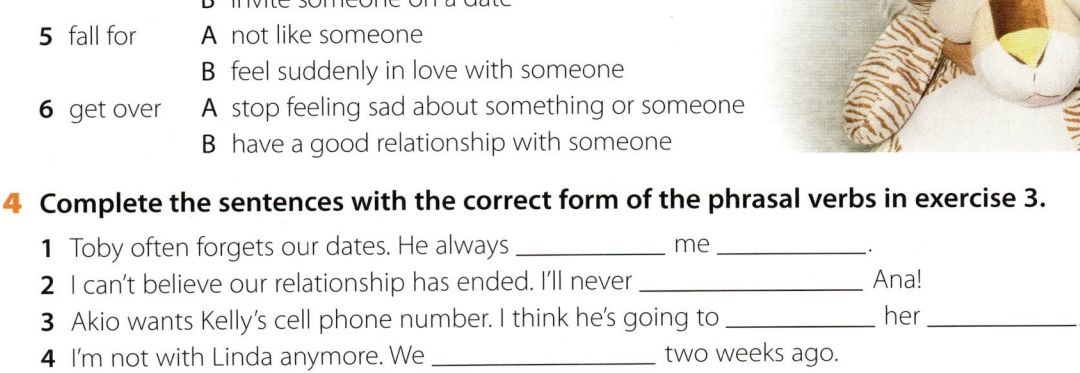

4 Complete the sentences with the correct form of the phrasal verbs in exercise 3.

1 Toby often forgets our dates. He always _____ me _____.
2 I can't believe our relationship has ended. I'll never _____ Ana!
3 Akio wants Kelly's cell phone number. I think he's going to _____ her _____.
4 I'm not with Linda anymore. We _____ two weeks ago.
5 Adam can't stop talking about Kelly. I think he's _____ her.
6 Olivia used to _____ with Tom, but she's with Ben now.

5

Grammar

1 Read the chart. Look at the **bold** verbs. Change the affirmative forms into the negative.

lives → *doesn't live*

Present and past tenses

Simple present	• Facts, permanent situations, present habits and states	– Jens **lives** in Germany.
Present continuous	• Actions in progress now, temporary present situations	– Two years later, we're still **going** out.
Simple past	• Finished past actions, past states	– Jens and I **met** on a beach.
Past continuous	• Actions in progress in the past, temporary past actions	– I **was doing** my chores all morning.
Past continuous + simple past	• An action in progress, interrupted by a short action (linked with *when* or *while*)	– I **was talking** to friends *when* Isabel **walked** in. – *While* I **was talking** to friends, Isabel **walked** in.

Remember!

- We use *used to* + infinitive for repeated routines, actions, or states that existed in the past, but no longer exist now.
  – I **used to make** an effort before a first date.

Language reference pages 62–63

2 Circle the correct alternatives.
1. My parents **lived / were living** in Paris when they **met / were meeting**.
2. Thirty years ago, people **used to write / were writing** more letters.
3. I often **feel / was feeling** nervous before a first date.
4. Lucia **is going / goes** out with Alvaro at the moment.
5. While Sara **waited / was waiting** for her train, a man on the platform **asked / was asking** her out.

3 Complete the sentences with the correct form of the verbs in parentheses. Use the simple present, present continuous, simple past, or past continuous.
1. Aaron _____ with Amy last night. (**break up**)
2. Right now, they _____ TV. (**watch**)
3. I _____ for a friend at the movie theater when I first _____ Luke. (**wait, see**)
4. Ella and David usually _____ each other every Saturday. (**meet**)
5. At ten o'clock this morning, we _____ chores. (**do**)

4 Read the *Language extra*. Write questions for the answers in the dialogue.

Alice	Who _were you talking to_, Joe?
Joe	Um … I was talking to Becky.
Alice	Who's Becky? How (1) _____?
Joe	I know her through my brother.
Alice	Did (2) _____?
Joe	No, I didn't use to go out with her!
Alice	When (3) _____?
Joe	I met her last summer at a party.
Alice	And why (4) _____?
Joe	I don't know why she's looking at me!

Language extra

- We normally form questions in the simple present and simple past with the auxiliary verb *do* + infinitive.
  – Where **does** Jens **live**?
  – Where **did** Beatriz **meet** Jens?
  – **Did** she **use to** make an effort?
- With *be* and continuous tenses, we do not use *do*.
  – **Am** I still upset?
  – What **were** you **doing** when Isabel walked in?

Relationships

Future forms

will + infinitive	• Talking about the future, expressing decisions made at that moment	– I'**ll get** over him. – I think I'**ll eat** out tonight.
be + going to + infinitive	• Expressing intentions, making predictions based on present evidence	– I'**m going to visit** him in Germany. – You'**re going to have** a great vacation.
Present continuous	• Talking about confirmed plans and personal arrangements	– We'**re going** to the same college this fall.

Language reference page 56

5 Circle the correct alternatives.

> **New Message**   Profile   Friends   Messages
>
> Hi Sally,
>
> It was great to meet you at school yesterday. Thanks for helping me on my first day! Which classes are you **(1) choosing / going to choose**? I don't think **(2) I'll pick / 'm picking** Art because I'm terrible at it. But **(3) I'm definitely going to study / 'm definitely studying** French – it's my best subject. Some students told me **(4) they're going / will go** to a party at Matt's house on Saturday. If you're planning to go, **(5) I'm going to see / 'll see** you there! **(6) I will go / 'm going** to the movies on Thursday – do you want to come?
>
> Cody

6 Look at Sally's calendar. Complete and answer the questions with the correct future forms.

MON 5	TUE 6	WED 7	THU 8	FRI 9
back to school	7 p.m. play volleyball		8 p.m. movies with Cody ☺	
SAT 10			**SUN 11**	
go to Matt's party with Emma and Lydia				

1. **A** What's Sally doing on Tuesday evening?
   B She _____.
2. **A** Who _____ to the movies with on Thursday?
   B She _____.
3. **A** Where _____ on Saturday?
   B She _____.
4. **A** _____ there with Cody?
   B No, she _____. She _____.

7 Complete the sentences with appropriate future forms. Use the verbs in parentheses.

It _'s going to snow_ today – look at the color of the sky! (**snow**)

1. When I'm older, I _____ a year abroad. (**spend**)
2. Next Tuesday, we _____ to the theater. (**go**)
3. How can I tell Mel how I feel? I know, I _____ her a letter! (**write**)
4. I don't feel well. I think I _____ home now. (**go**)
5. Joe _____ college next fall. (**start**)

Grammar   Get it right

Correct the errors in these sentences.

1. "When did Max and Ana broke up?"
   "Three weeks ago."
2. Lisa is go to speak to Jorge later.
3. They was relaxing in the backyard.
4. "I don't want to go to the party alone."
   "I'm going with you."
5. What time are they arrive?
6. We use to spend a lot of time together.

1 Home Sweet Home

Reading

Stage 1 Get ready!

1 Read the *Reading strategy*. Follow steps 1–3. What do you think the brochure is about?

> **Reading strategy**
>
> **Using previous knowledge**
> 1 Read the title and look at the pictures.
> 2 Decide what the topic of the text is.
> 3 Use your knowledge to predict what the text will be about and which words may appear.

2 Look at the brochure below. Circle the benefits you think the brochure will mention about the building.

> eco-friendly • isolated • low-cost • modern • natural • traditional

3 Skim the brochure. Which benefits from exercise 2 can you find?

TinyDwelling homes for the 21st century

1 In today's consumer world, we've never had so much, yet it seems we've never been so unsatisfied. The cost of housing has been rising for decades, and the cost to the planet has been enormous, too. But there is a way to live a simpler, greener, and more affordable life: buy a TinyDwelling home!

2 TinyDwelling homes are very small, yet comfortable houses at affordable prices. Each charming TinyDwelling home has a contemporary design and includes a living room, kitchen, bathroom, upstairs sleeping area, and convenient storage space. TinyDwelling homes are cheap to run and eco-friendly, too. All you need is a small heater to keep your house warm in chilly weather, and solar panels in order to provide light and electricity.

3 TinyDwelling is part of the small-living movement that began in the late 1990s. Back then, a growing number of people began to live in very small homes. They wanted to downsize their possessions, living space, and energy costs, so as to lead more ecologically-friendly lives. But the small-living movement really took off after the economic crisis of 2008, when many people realized that they couldn't afford to own and maintain large homes.

4 Lizzy Morrison, a small-living enthusiast, started TinyDwelling homes in 2008 to cater to the needs of these people. Since then, Lizzy has been designing and building homes nonstop, and TinyDwelling homes have become so popular that thousands of people have bought one. And Lizzy hasn't only been designing and building houses. She has also been teaching people how to build them. Simply buy the plans and materials so that you can build your own home, and save even more money!

5 *"Our old home was spacious and comfortable, but it was also old-fashioned and expensive to maintain. We've always wanted a greener lifestyle, so when I lost my job, we decided to downsize. The TinyDwelling concept really appealed to us. We bought the plans for a Kicsi house and attended Lizzy's fantastic workshop in order to learn how to build it. Despite a bruised thumb and a few other minor injuries, we successfully put together our own house and have been living in it for eighteen months. We've had such a satisfying life since we moved in that we've been asking ourselves why we didn't do it years ago!"*

Doug, Milwaukee, Wisconsin

TinyDwelling homes

Size of TinyDwelling house	Cost of plans	Building costs (if built by TinyDwelling)	Building costs (if built by you)
Bijou: 25 m²	$400	$39,500	$17,000
Kicsi: 35 m²	$839	$47,000	$21,000
Lilla: 50 m²	$912	$51,000	$24,500

Focus on false friends

4 Find these words in the text. Circle the correct definitions.

1 realized (line 23) — became aware / carried out
2 large (line 24) — big / wide
3 attended (line 40) — paid attention to / were at an event

False friends list pages 60–61

Home Sweet Home

Stage 2 Read and understand

5 🔊 **1.03** Read the brochure again. Choose the correct answers.

1 The text implies that in today's world …
   A everybody wants to save the planet.
   B people don't have a lot of possessions.
   C people are damaging the environment.
   D poor people are very unsatisfied.
   E people with a lot of possessions are happier.

2 *TinyDwelling* houses …
   A don't need a heater.
   B aren't cheap to heat.
   C come with solar panels.
   D don't use electricity.
   E can get cold without a heater.

3 The small-living movement …
   A believes in having a lot of possessions.
   B believes that small houses are good for the environment.
   C consists of people who can't afford to live in big houses.
   D doesn't include *TinyDwelling* homes.
   E was started by Lizzy Morrison in the late 1990s.

4 Lizzy Morrison …
   A teaches people to build homes.
   B saves money when she buys the plans and materials.
   C only teaches people how to build the *Kicsi* house.
   D buys plans to build new homes.
   E has never taught a workshop before.

5 You need the plans for a *TinyDwelling* house if you …
   A don't want to build the house yourself.
   B have asked *TinyDwellings* to build the house.
   C are going to pay $39,500 for the Bijou house.
   D are planning to build the house yourself.
   E need a bigger home than the Kicsi house.

6 Doug says the Kicsi house …
   A took eighteen months to put together.
   B is very pleasant to live in.
   C is what they wanted years ago.
   D caused him serious injuries.
   E is spacious and comfortable.

6 Match definitions 1–6 with words or phrases in the brochure.

1 a place where you can keep things (paragraph 2) _____
2 reduce (paragraph 3) _____
3 keep something in good condition (paragraph 3) _____
4 continuously (paragraph 4) _____
5 a class, often for learning a practical skill (paragraph 5) _____
6 where the skin is marked by an injury (paragraph 5) _____

Vocabulary

Adjectives: home and place

1 Read the advertisement and look at the photos. Match the description with the correct photo.

Apartment FOR SALE!

This **contemporary**, **spacious** apartment is perfect for city life! It's close to stores and restaurants, and is in a **convenient** location for public transportation, too. It's **warm** and **cozy** in the winter, with low energy bills. What's more, this **charming** apartment comes at a very **affordable** price!

☎ For more details, call
212.555.4200

2 Match the **bold** adjectives in exercise 1 with their opposites 1–7 below.

1 chilly _____
2 unpleasant _____
3 old-fashioned _____
4 expensive _____
5 uninviting _____
6 inconvenient _____
7 cramped _____

3 Circle the correct alternatives.

1 My bedroom is tiny with lots of furniture so it's **affordable** / **cramped**.
2 The house isn't near any stores, which is a little **charming** / **inconvenient**.
3 We don't have much money so it's hard to find something that's **affordable** / **chilly** at the moment.
4 The living room looked very **cozy** / **chilly** with sofas and plenty of cushions.
5 Our home is **spacious** / **old-fashioned** – we haven't decorated it for years.
6 The apartment was **unpleasant** / **warm** – the furniture was old and dirty.

Focus on phrasal verbs

4 Write the infinitive form of the red phrasal verbs in these sentences. Match them with the definitions below.

> make something by fitting parts together • start living in a new place • become successful • provide the things that a person needs

1 The school **caters to** children from the age of three to eighteen.
2 Luis has just **moved in**. He's unpacking boxes this weekend.
3 We **put** the furniture **together** over the weekend.
4 Your idea is great. It's going to **take off**!

Word list
affordable
charming
chilly
convenient
contemporary
cozy
cramped
expensive
inconvenient
old-fashioned
spacious
uninviting
unpleasant
warm

cater to
move in
put together
take off

Home Sweet Home 1

Language workshop

> **so ... that / such ... that**
>
> - To introduce the result of something, we can use *so* + adjective / adverb + *that*
>   – Lizzy's homes are **so popular that** thousands of people have bought one.
> - Or we can use *such* (+ *a / an*) + adjective + noun + *that*
>   – It was **such a small house that** they could transport it on wheels.
>
> **Language reference page 65**

5 Complete the sentences with *so* or *such*.

1. Energy bills are now _____ high that many people struggle to pay them.
2. It was _____ a chilly room that I had to keep the heat on all day.
3. The apartment had _____ old-fashioned furniture that I didn't like it.
4. He was moving _____ often that he needed a house on wheels.

6 Join the sentences with the **bold** words.

Molly's room is cramped. She can't put anything else in it. (so ... that)
Molly's room is so cramped that she can't put anything else in it.

1. It was an expensive house. We knew we couldn't afford it. (such ... that)
   _____
2. Eva's new job was far away. She had to move. (so ... that)
   _____
3. It was a great idea. I had to tell everyone about it. (such ... that)
   _____
4. I was working hard. I never saw my friends. (so ... that)
   _____

> **Conjunctions of purpose**
>
> - We use conjunctions of purpose to introduce reasons.
>
>   so (that) • in order to • to • so as to
>
> – People often move around the country **so that** they can find work.
> – I sold my house **to / in order to / so as to** save money.
>
> **Language reference page 65**

7 Complete rules 1 and 2 with the correct conjunctions of purpose.

1. _____, _____, and _____ go before an infinitive verb.
2. _____ goes before a subject and a verb.

8 Complete each sentence with a conjunction of purpose.

1. You should buy a heater _____ your house doesn't get cold.
2. Kate has been looking online _____ find a new apartment.
3. I'm going to bed early _____ I'll be fresh for the exam tomorrow.
4. He wore his new suit _____ look professional at the job interview.

Vocabulary   Get it right

Correct the errors in these sentences.

This unit
1. My house is cramped because it's close to stores.
2. I bought a solar panel so that save money on bills.
3. The apartment was such chilly that there was ice on the windows!

Previous unit
4. My parents do a big effort on my birthday.
5. This exercise is hard but I'm doing the best.
6. Lisa is sad about the argument, but she'll get on it.

Grammar

Stage 1 Get ready!

1 Read the chart. Look at the **bold** verbs. Write the verbs in the first person singular.

> **Present perfect simple and continuous**
>
> Past actions or situations that are continuing now, have present results, or finished recently.
>
> **Present perfect simple**
> - Achievements and results
>   – Doug **has built** his own home.
> - Permanent situations
>   – Lizzy **has lived** here since 2007.
> - How often we have done something
>   – He**'s seen** two apartments this week.
>
> **Remember!**
> - We do not use present perfect tenses for finished past time periods or actions.
>   – Maria lived in Paris from 2002 until 2007. ✓
>   – Maria has lived in Paris from 2002 until 2007. ✗
>
> **Present perfect continuous**
> - Processes and durations (of temporary actions or situations)
>   – For the past year, Alan **has been living** in a mobile home.
> - Situations that finished very recently, or may be unfinished (with present evidence)
>   – Paolo **has been cooking** fish. (I can still smell it.)
>   – **Have** you **been decorating your house**? (You have paint on your clothes.)
>
> **Remember!**
> - We often use this tense with "up to now" time expressions.
>   *recently, lately, all day, since Friday, this week, for the past year, etc.*
> - We do not use it to say how often we have done something.
>   – She's been looking at houses three times this week. ✗
> - We do not normally use continuous tenses with stative verbs. (*be, have, know* …)
>   – We've known about *TinyDwellings* for years. ✓
>   – We've been knowing about *TinyDwellings* for years. ✗
>
> **Language reference pages 64–65**

Stage 2 Practice

2 Circle the correct alternatives.

Zac   Hi, Mom! I (1) **moved / 've moved** into my new apartment.
Mom   That's great! When can I come see it?
Zac   Well, it's very dirty – I (2) **didn't have / haven't had** time to clean it yet. I'll call you in a few days.
Mom   But Zac, we (3) **didn't see / haven't seen** you for weeks!
Zac   That isn't true! I (4) **came / have come** home for dinner last Sunday.
Mom   No, Zac. You (5) **have been / were** here the Sunday before that. And you only (6) **have stayed / stayed** for an hour!

3 Complete the sentences with the words in parentheses. Use the present perfect continuous.

Julia *hasn't been going out with* her friends lately. (**not go out with**)

1 I _____ at college since the fall. (**study**)
2 You _____ my phone calls recently. (**not answer**)
3 Where _____ since May? (**Dan / live**)
4 Sara _____ tea this week. (**not drink**)
5 How long _____ their rooms? (**Tom and Ben / clean**)
6 Leo _____ a lot of time in the library lately. (**spend**)

Home Sweet Home 1

4 Complete the dialogue with the verbs below. Use the present perfect continuous.

~~do~~ • look • read • spend • study • tell • think • watch

Lucy Hi! What _have_ you _been doing_ this afternoon?
Emma I have an exam tomorrow, so I (1) _____. But I (2) _____ at furniture online, too. You know I (3) _____ about buying furniture for my new apartment.
Lucy Yes, you (4) _____ everyone about it for months! And you (5) _____ hours in furniture stores, too!
Emma Well, anyway, I (6) _____ about Casulo furniture.
Lucy Oh? What's that?
Emma It's furniture in a box! There's a bed, a desk, stools, a closet, and lots of storage.
Lucy All that in one box?
Emma Yes! And I (7) _____ a video about it online. You can put everything together in less than ten minutes.
Lucy Wow! It sounds great!

5 Circle the correct alternatives.
1 My legs and arms are hurting. I've **exercised / been exercising** all morning.
2 Amy! Why are all your friends here? **Have you had / Have you been having** a party?
3 They **haven't decorated / haven't been decorating** the house since they bought it.
4 Since 2010, I **have lived / have been living** in three different countries.
5 **Have you met / Have you been meeting** my brother? Ana, this is Luke.

6 Complete the sentences with the verbs in parentheses. Use the present perfect simple or the present perfect continuous.
1 I don't know where your cell phone is. I _____ it anywhere. (**not see**)
2 Toby _____ in the kitchen all morning. (**cook**)
3 We _____ for our exams, so we haven't done any chores. (**study**)
4 Jenny is happy because she _____ her first home. (**buy**)
5 They _____ the house for a long time. (**not paint**)
6 The doctor says I _____ my leg. (**break**)

Grammar   Get it right

Correct the errors in these sentences.

This unit
1 My brother has moved last month.
2 I am living in London for seven years.
3 You've watched TV all morning. I think you should stop now.

Previous unit
4 He was watching the TV when he was hearing the phone ring.
5 You did use to live in Cairo.
6 We're meet this evening at 8 p.m.

2 The World of Work

Reading

Stage 1 Get ready!

1 Look at the photos and the title. What do you think the magazine article is about?
2 Skim the article and check your answer to exercise 1.
3 Find these words and phrases in the article. What do you think they mean?

1 seek your fortune (v)   3 economic slump (n)   5 newcomers (n)
2 booming (adj)   4 mere (adj)   6 disheartened (adj)

The Brazilian dream

By Elliott White

Since the Portuguese came to seek their fortune in 1500, Brazil, with its vast terrain and abundant natural resources, has been seen by many as a land of opportunity. In the 19th and early 20th centuries, hundreds of thousands of migrants from Europe and Japan came to Brazil, hoping that they could earn a living from agriculture. Then, in the 1950s, many workers came from the Middle East to take up work in Brazil's growing industrial sector.

Now, in the early 21st century, Brazil is once again proving irresistible to foreign workers. Its booming economy is creating job vacancies in many sectors. For example, oil and gas exploration have grown rapidly. As host of the FIFA World Cup in 2014 and the Olympic Games in 2016, Brazil has had to invest heavily in its infrastructure. The country's mining industry is also thriving, due to a strong trading partnership with China.

Meanwhile, the worldwide economic slump, in the US in particular, has contributed to Brazil's popularity with foreign workers. The US economy grew by a mere 2.9% in 2010, compared with Brazil's impressive growth rate of 7.5% that year. The current US unemployment rate is 9.1%, but in Brazil, 57% of employers say there aren't enough workers to fill vacancies. This might account for the thousands of Americans who have moved to Brazil in search of work.

It isn't always easy to move abroad for work. Newcomers must be hard-working, reliable, and adaptable in order to secure lasting employment. For many, learning a new language and customs must be challenging, too. Anyone planning a new life in Brazil should think these things over carefully. They must not forget that they will be far from home and won't be able to see their family or friends very often.

A Japanese cotton picker working in Brazil, 1939

Isabelle Fisher moved to Brazil from the US last year. She tells us why she relocated:

"I'm an aviation engineer, but I lost my job in Denver two years ago. I didn't get any of the new jobs I went for and felt disheartened. So when a friend told me there were a lot of vacancies in Brazil, I applied for a job. Now, I work for an airline company near Sao Paulo."

It must have been hard to leave your family and friends behind.

"It was. I remember feeling unhappy at first, mainly because I couldn't communicate with people. I should have taken language classes before I left. But life here is terrific now. Brazilian people are very outgoing and I've made some great friends. I can speak a little Portuguese, too. Without my friend's advice, I might have missed out on this great opportunity!"

How long will you stay?

"I may stay a few years. I'm pretty flexible. Who knows what might happen?"

Focus on false friends

4 Find these words in the text. Circle the correct definitions.

1 in particular (line 19)   *in private / especially*
2 current (line 22)   *happening now / common*
3 terrific (line 53)   *extremely good / terrifying*

False friends list pages 60–61

14

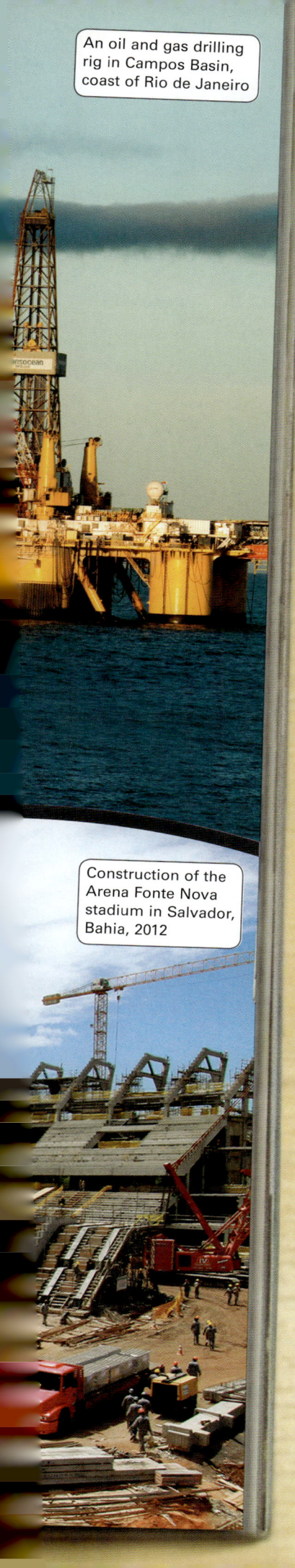

An oil and gas drilling rig in Campos Basin, coast of Rio de Janeiro

The World of Work 2

Stage 2 Read and understand

Reading strategy

Multiple choice questions
1 Read the text carefully.
2 Read the questions. Find the relevant parts of the text. It may help to look for synonyms of the key words from the questions.
3 Remember that the text must state or imply the correct answer. Don't rely on your own knowledge.

5 🔊 **1.04** Read the *Reading strategy* above. Follow steps 1–3. Choose the correct answers for questions 1–6 below.

1 People may move to Brazil because …
  A they have a lot of money.
  B they want to make money there.
  C there are 1,500 opportunities in Brazil.
  D it's a vast country.
  E it costs a fortune to go to Portugal.

2 Japanese migrants …
  A wanted jobs in farming.
  B went to work in the Middle East.
  C couldn't get jobs in Europe.
  D are now finding work in the US.
  E never had the opportunity to go to Brazil.

3 Brazil …
  A doesn't have any oil at the moment.
  B needs a stronger mining industry.
  C has spent a lot on its infrastructure.
  D hasn't developed its infrastructure.
  E doesn't have vacancies in its industrial sector.

4 Brazil …
  A is experiencing an economic slump.
  B has 57% more workers than the US.
  C doesn't have any workers from the US.
  D needs more employees in its companies.
  E has 57% American workers.

5 Newcomers to Brazil need to …
  A have the right qualities in order to get lasting jobs.
  B have a lot of money in order to live comfortably.
  C learn the language and customs.
  D see their families very often.
  E find a job before they arrive in Brazil.

6 Isabelle Fisher moved to Brazil because …
  A her company sent her there.
  B she had family and friends in Brazil.
  C she didn't want a job in Denver.
  D she wanted to learn Portuguese.
  E she got a job there.

Construction of the Arena Fonte Nova stadium in Salvador, Bahia, 2012

6 Find the figures and periods 1–4 in the article. Match them with facts A–D.

1 9.1% ____
2 21st century ____
3 7.5% ____
4 19th and 20th centuries ____

A how much Brazil's wealth increased in 2010
B the number of Americans without a job in 2011
C when workers from Europe and East Asia migrated to Brazil
D the time when many workers came to Brazil from the US

7 Read statements 1–3. According to the article, which are true?
1 Foreign workers have helped Brazil's economy.
2 Brazil's current influx of foreign workers is due to its strong economy.
3 Americans are choosing Brazil because they can learn the language easily.
  A 1 and 2.   B 3 only.   C 1 and 3.

Vocabulary

Adjectives: personal qualities

1 Read the advertisement below. What services does OzOpportunities offer?

Summer jobs with OzOpportunities!

Are you in college and over 18? Do you want to work in Australia during your summer break? Look no further! OzOpportunities' **considerate** and friendly team helps students find jobs and accommodations in Australia's cities. OzOpportunities even organizes your social life!

OzOpportunities is looking for **adaptable** young people who are ready for a new experience. You must be **energetic** and **reliable**, always prepared to work long hours, and able to arrive at work on time. And it helps if you're **sociable**: with OzOpportunities, you're going to make a lot of new friends!

2 Look at the **bold** adjectives in exercise 1. Which adjective has an opposite which begins with the prefix *in-*?

3 Read the sentences. Replace the **bold** words with words from the text in exercise 1.
  1 Paul is a very **outgoing** person and always talks to new people. _____
  2 I can trust my workers because they're very **dependable**. _____
  3 You're so **hard-working**! You've been helping in your dad's store all weekend! _____
  4 Sam hates working on weekends. He needs to be more **flexible** if he wants to find a job. _____
  5 When I first arrived in Australia, Emily helped me a lot. She's a very **kind** girl. _____

4 Circle the correct alternatives.
  1 Kenji's boss trusts him because he knows he's **adaptable / reliable**.
  2 Lucy is a popular girl because she's **sociable / hard-working** and friendly.
  3 I was nervous in my new job, but the other workers were **kind / energetic** to me.
  4 A bar worker needs to be **flexible / outgoing** – you have to talk to a lot of people!
  5 Roberto works hard and is never late. He's very **dependable / considerate**.

Focus on phrasal verbs

5 Write the infinitive form of the red phrasal verbs in these sentences. Match them with the definitions below.

> provide an explanation for • begin doing (a job) •
> consider something carefully •
> go away from a place without taking something with you

  1 I'd like more time to **think** things **over** before I decide.
  2 Last year Adam **took up** a position in his father's business.
  3 I'm at the airport, but I've **left** my passport **behind**!
  4 William used to eat very unhealthily which **accounted for** his weight gain.

Word list
adaptable
considerate
dependable
energetic
flexible
hard-working
kind
outgoing
reliable
sociable

account for
leave behind
take up
think over

The World of Work 2

Language workshop

Negative prefixes

- We can make many adjectives negative by adding the correct negative prefix.

Prefix	Positive adjective	Negative adjective	Prefix	Positive adjective	Negative adjective
un-	employed	unemployed	in-	flexible	inflexible
il-	logical	illogical	ir-	resistible	irresistible
im-	possible	impossible	dis-	organized	disorganized

Language reference page 67

6 Complete the sentences with the negative form of the adjectives below. Use a dictionary to help you.

friendly • honest • practical • responsible • significant

1 No one can call Australians _____. They've been so kind to me.
2 Not telling your boss you're going to be late for work is _____.
3 It was _____ to move our furniture from the US for a short time.
4 Never lie about your work experience. It's _____.
5 I'm so happy in my new job. My initial worries now seem _____.

Easily-confused words

- Words that have similar spellings or similar meanings can be easily confused.
  remember / remind
  – You must **remember** to make an appointment. = You must not forget to do this.
  – You must **remind** me to make an appointment. = You must tell me to do this because I might forget.

Language reference page 67

7 Complete the sentences with the correct form of the **bold** words.

remember / remind
1 She _____ him to go to the meeting.
2 He _____ to reply to the email.

say / tell
3 Could you _____ me the time, please?
4 Sorry, I didn't hear you. What did you _____?

borrow / lend
5 Can I _____ your new jacket tomorrow?
6 OK, I'll _____ it to you. But I need it back for the weekend.

lose / miss
7 I've _____ the tickets for the movie theater.
8 We're going to _____ the movie!

earn / win
9 I don't _____ much money in my job.
10 One day I might _____ the lottery!

Vocabulary   Get it right

Correct the errors in these sentences.

This unit
1 Leo is very kind. He can change his working hours.
2 It's unpolite to ignore people when they speak to you.
3 Did you remind to go to the bank?

Previous unit
4 The workshop takes off all levels of ability.
5 The exam was such difficult that I'm sure I failed.
6 People migrate so as find work in other countries.

Grammar

Stage ❶ Get ready!

1 Read the chart. Look back at the text on page 14. Find examples of these modals. Which categories do they belong to?

Modals

Modal verbs

Ability
- Japanese migrants believed they **could** make money in Brazil.
- You **can** stay with us while you look for an apartment.
- If I finish my degree, I **will be able to** get a good job.

Possibility and deduction
- I **could** / **may** / **might** look for a job in Spain.
- It **must** be hard / **can't** be easy to move abroad.

Advice, obligation, prohibition
- Before you move to a country, you **should** check its current employment statistics.
- Newcomers **must** / **have to** be hard-working.
- You **must not** drive without a license.

Lack of obligation
- I **don't have to** work tomorrow because it's a holiday.

Modal perfects

Possibility in the past
- could / might / may have + past participle
  - I'm sorry I didn't enter the competition. I **could** / **may** / **might have won** a car!

Deduction in the past
- must have, can't have + past participle
  - It **must have been** hard / **can't have been** easy to leave family and friends behind.

Regret or criticism in the past
- should have + past participle
  - I **shouldn't have waited** so long to find a new job.

Language reference pages 66–67

Stage ❷ Practice

2 Circle the correct alternatives.

1. Alice likes working with children, so she **might** / **must** become a teacher.
2. It's Saturday tomorrow, so I **don't have to** / **shouldn't** get up early.
3. When Pete finishes college, he **couldn't** / **'ll be able to** get a good job.
4. If you're feeling unwell, perhaps you **shouldn't** / **must not** go out tonight.
5. She has two exams tomorrow, so she **can** / **must** be nervous.
6. When you move to a new country, you **might** / **have to** be adaptable.

3 Complete the sentences with the correct modal verb.

Lawyers _must_ have a college degree.

1. You _____ drive through a red light. It's illegal.
2. If you're worried about the exam, you _____ tell your teacher.
3. I _____ do my homework. I've already finished it!
4. We _____ get on the plane because we don't have our tickets.

4 Choose the correct answers to complete the sentences.

Sorry, everyone. I can't find the tickets. I ____ left them behind.
(A) might have   B should have   C can't have

1. Toby's been in Australia for ten months now. He ____ found a job there!
   A shouldn't have   B can't have   C must have
2. Emma's shoes are hurting her feet. She ____ worn more comfortable ones.
   A couldn't have   B should have   C might have
3. Oh, dear. Joe is back from his date early. It ____ gone well!
   A could have   B may have   C can't have
4. I don't know if Mr. White is still in his office. He ____ gone home already.
   A may have   B must have   C should have

The World of Work 2

5 Complete the sentences with appropriate modal perfects. Use positive and negative forms. There may be more than one correct answer.

You _can't have_ finished the book already! You only started it yesterday!

1 It wasn't smart to cycle without a helmet. You _____ hurt yourself.
2 Eddie _____ been honest. Now people don't trust him anymore.
3 I don't know where my sister is. She _____ gone shopping.
4 You worked so hard for that test. You _____ passed it!
5 The flight from Lisbon is sometimes delayed. It _____ arrived yet.

6 Read the text. Complete it with the modal perfect form of the verbs below.

might move • must make • may be • couldn't go • can't recognize • should say • must become • could work

People have often wondered what happened to Rob after we left high school. We knew he _couldn't have gone_ to college, because he failed all his classes and didn't graduate. My mother thought he **(1)** _____ for his parents in their store. I thought he **(2)** _____ to a different state, because he hated Florida. Then, three months ago, I saw him on TV. At first I thought I **(3)** _____ a mistake. But it was him! He was holding a Grammy, so I realized that he **(4)** _____ a musician. Last month I saw him again getting out of a limo at the airport! There were screaming girls everywhere – they **(5)** _____ his fans. But he walked right past me. He **(6)** _____ me. Otherwise he would have said "hello", wouldn't he? Maybe I **(7)** _____ "hello" to him …

7 Complete the sentences with appropriate modal verbs or modal perfects. There may be more than one correct answer.

1 I _____ babysit my little brother tonight. My parents are going out.
2 Mel _____ thought over all her options. She made a bad choice.
3 Tom _____ go to college, but he hasn't decided yet.
4 You _____ seen Kelly yesterday. She's in Italy.
5 Alex _____ go to the party because his cousins were visiting.
6 I _____ met Tom before, but I'm not sure.
7 You _____ text while driving. It's illegal.

Grammar Get it right

Correct the errors in these sentences.

This unit
1 When I worked in a café, I must wear a uniform. It was the rule.
2 Rafael was rude to me. He should apologized.
3 I could have given you the answer. I didn't know it myself.

Previous unit
4 For the past month, Jane has been live close to her work.
5 I've been knowing your family for many years.
6 Tom and Al have worked together from 2008 until 2011.

3 Sports Heroes

Reading

Stage 1 Get ready!

1. Look at the photos. Who is this woman?
2. Skim the article and check your answer to exercise 1.
3. Find these words in the article. What do you think they mean?
   1. formidable *(adj)*
   2. ruthless *(adj)*
   3. try-out *(n)*
   4. product endorsement *(n)*

SPORT — Soccer | Cycling | Tennis | Athletics | Search

Pele in a skirt

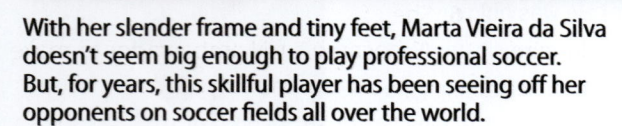

With her slender frame and tiny feet, Marta Vieira da Silva doesn't seem big enough to play professional soccer. But, for years, this skillful player has been seeing off her opponents on soccer fields all over the world.

5 Marta's appearance hides formidable skill. Standing at just 1.63m tall, she looks too petite to take on her more well-built opponents. Her cute smile hides a ruthless ability to see opportunities on the field where others can't – to change direction suddenly, surprising everyone with her
10 moves, and then shoot the ball into the net.

Fans have even compared Marta to Brazilian soccer heroes, Ronaldinho and Kaka. Some call her "Pele in a skirt".

Marta was born in northeast Brazil in 1986. As a child, her talent for the "beautiful game" emerged on the streets near
15 her home after her brothers had agreed to let their slim little sister join in with their games. But Marta's rise to soccer fame wasn't easy.

Life was difficult. Marta's mother brought her children up alone because their father had left home when Marta was
20 little. There had never been enough money to go around. Marta's mother wanted to help her daughter succeed, but had never had any experience in the soccer world before.

In her hometown of Dois Riachos, Marta was the only female player on the local team. Before she could play,
25 she had to prove that she was powerful enough, because most people believed women were too weak to play soccer. But Marta's ingenuity and determination were obvious. Even her try-out for her first professional team, in Rio de Janeiro,
30 was a test of endurance. She had to play right after she had traveled from her home by bus for three days.

Marta's story reflects many of the problems in women's professional soccer. Due to a reduction in sponsors' funding, several of Marta's former soccer clubs in Brazil, Sweden, and
35 the US have now closed down. Today, Marta has product endorsement contracts with several large companies, but her earnings still aren't high enough to match male players' salaries.

Yet Marta's career history seems too good to be true. By
40 2008, after four years in Sweden, she had scored 111 goals in 103 games. She had helped Brazil win the silver medal in the 2004 and 2008 Olympic Games women's soccer event. She had also been named FIFA Women's World Player of the Year five times.

45 Today, Marta wants to use her fame to help others. In 2010, the United Nations appointed her a goodwill ambassador. In this role, she encourages women to stand up for their rights and to fight against poverty. Her high profile is also helping women's soccer, which is rapidly becoming more
50 popular. Thanks to Marta, no one can call soccer a man's sport anymore.

Focus on false friends

4. Find these words in the text. Circle the correct definitions.
   1. prove (line 25)   *try, taste / show something is true*
   2. ingenuity (line 27)   *lack of experience / quality of being clever, original, and inventive*
   3. appointed (line 46)   *gave a role to (someone) / noted down*

False friends list pages 60–61

Sports Heroes

Stage 2 Read and understand

5 🔊 **1.05** Read the article again. Choose the correct answers.

1 Marta Vieira da Silva …
   A is too small to play soccer.
   B isn't skillful enough to beat her opponents.
   C isn't as big as other female soccer players.
   D can't see many opportunities on the soccer field.
   E believes her smile helps her score goals.

2 Marta's brothers …
   A have compared her to Ronaldinho and Kaka.
   B let her play soccer with them.
   C made her wear a skirt.
   D never played soccer with her.
   E thought that soccer was too difficult for Marta.

3 Marta's mother …
   A wanted to move to Rio de Janeiro.
   B had played soccer when she was young.
   C didn't have a lot of experience in soccer.
   D didn't want Marta to play soccer.
   E left home when Marta was little.

4 In Dois Riachos, Marta …
   A grew up without her father.
   B didn't have enough money to play soccer.
   C was too skinny to play soccer.
   D chose a few women to play on her soccer team.
   E didn't think she was powerful enough to play soccer.

5 Marta …
   A played for her first professional team for only three days.
   B didn't live far from her first professional team.
   C traveled by bus to three countries.
   D has played for teams that no longer exist.
   E earns as much as male soccer stars.

6 She…
   A became a UN ambassador to make women's soccer popular.
   B has never played at the Olympics.
   C has scored 111 goals for Brazil.
   D stopped playing soccer in 2010.
   E helped Brazil's Olympic women's soccer team come second twice.

Reading strategy

Answering in your own words
1 Read the question carefully. Underline the key words.
2 Find the relevant part of the text and read it carefully.
3 Write these ideas in a different way. Do not repeat the text exactly.
4 When you have finished writing, check your grammar and spelling.

6 Read the *Reading strategy* above. Follow steps 1–4. Answer the questions in your own words.

1 Why does Marta's physical appearance confuse people?
   _____
   _____

2 Why do some people call Marta "Pele in a skirt"?
   _____
   _____

3 How does Marta earn her money?
   _____
   _____

Vocabulary

Adjectives: physical attributes

1 Read the webpage about volleyball. Complete the text with the words below.

> tiny • good-looking • powerful • slim

2 Complete the chart with the correct synonyms and antonyms from the text. Use a dictionary to help you.

	Synonym	Antonym
cute	good-looking	1 _____
petite	2 _____	3 _____
slender	4 _____	5 _____
strong	6 _____	7 _____

3 Circle the correct alternatives.
1 A petite person can play volleyball. You don't have to be **weak / huge**!
2 Dan used to be **good-looking / overweight**, but now he's very slim.
3 I don't like my new haircut. I think I look **ugly / huge**!
4 After a month in the hospital, Luis still isn't strong enough to walk. He's very **weak / cute**.

4 Write a paragraph about a friend or a member of your family. Which physical attributes does he / she have to make him / her good at their sport? Use the adjectives in exercises 1, 2, and 3.

_____ is my friend / brother / sister, etc.
He's / She's (a / an) _____ and / but he's / she's very _____.
He / She is / isn't _____ or _____.
He / She is also _____ – definitely not _____.

Carlos is my friend. He's a basketball player and he's very fast. He's quite tall and …

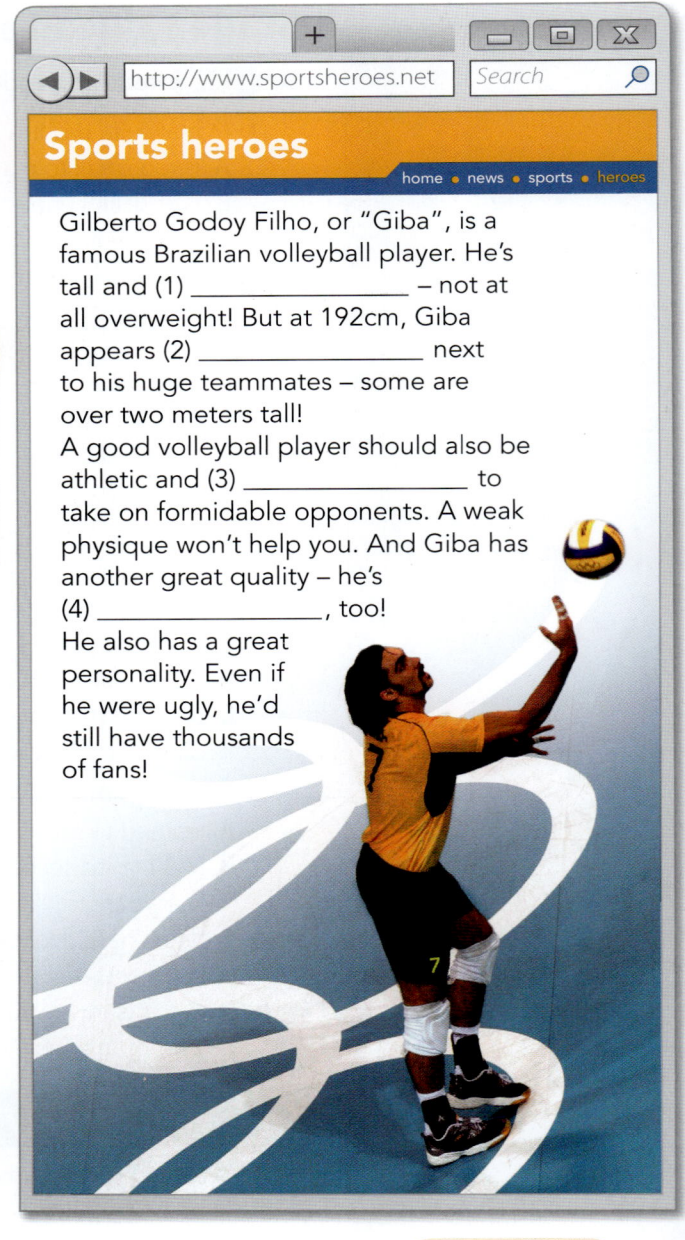

Sports heroes

http://www.sportsheroes.net

home • news • sports • heroes

Gilberto Godoy Filho, or "Giba", is a famous Brazilian volleyball player. He's tall and (1) _____ – not at all overweight! But at 192cm, Giba appears (2) _____ next to his huge teammates – some are over two meters tall!
A good volleyball player should also be athletic and (3) _____ to take on formidable opponents. A weak physique won't help you. And Giba has another great quality – he's (4) _____, too!
He also has a great personality. Even if he were ugly, he'd still have thousands of fans!

Focus on phrasal verbs

5 Write the infinitive form of the red phrasal verbs in these sentences. Match them with the definitions below.

> stop operating (of a business) • play against someone in a game or contest • defeat someone in a game / fight, etc. • care for a child until it is an adult

1 Alice **brought up** her grandchildren because their parents had to work abroad.
2 Olivia decided to **take on** her coach at tennis.
3 A lot of stores in our town have **closed down** due to the recession.
4 Roger Federer **saw off** several top players to win the tournament.

Word list
cute
good-looking
huge
overweight
petite
powerful
slender
slim
strong
tiny
ugly
weak

bring up
close down
see off
take on

Sports Heroes 3

Language workshop

too / not ... enough

- *too* + adjective / adverb (+ *to* + infinitive)
  – Her career seems **too good** to be true.
- *not* + adjective / adverb + *enough* (+ *to* + infinitive)
  – Marta does**n't** seem **big enough** to play soccer.

Remember!
- When we use a verb after *too* or *not ... enough*, we use the infinitive with *to*, never the gerund.

Language reference page 69

6 Rewrite the sentences with *too* or *not ... enough* and the words in parentheses.

Juan isn't old enough to play professional soccer. (**young**)
Juan is too young to play professional soccer.

1 I missed the game because I got up too late. (**early**)
_____

2 I wasn't fast enough to catch the bus. (**slow**)
_____

3 Amy is too short to play volleyball. (**tall**)
_____

4 This apartment is too small for a family of four. (**big**)
_____

5 He isn't slim enough to wear his old pants. (**overweight**)
_____

Noun suffixes (1)

- We can make nouns by adding suffixes to many verbs. Sometimes the spelling changes.

  agree → agree**ment** • determine → determin**ation** • confuse → confus**ion** • differ → differ**ence** • appear → appear**ance**

Language reference page 69

7 Complete the chart with the correct noun form of the verbs below.
Use a dictionary to help you.

~~advertise~~ • amuse • endure • explain • imitate • prefer • promote • tolerate

-ment	-ance	-ion	-ation	-ence
advertisement	_____	_____	_____	_____
_____	_____	_____	_____	_____

8 Complete the sentences with nouns from exercise 7.

1 Dad has just gotten a _____ at work. He's going to earn more money.
2 I'm happy to watch the game or see a movie. I don't have any _____.
3 Nowadays there is less _____ of sexism in sports.
4 You haven't done any homework for three weeks. What's the _____?

Vocabulary Get it right

Correct the errors in these sentences.

This unit
1 Ana is petite because she eats too much.
2 Be quiet! You're being noisy enough!
3 It's been a good meeting. Thank you for your participance.

Previous unit
4 Have you thought on your plans for the future?
5 James was insuccessful and didn't win the game.
6 I missed my ticket, so I couldn't go to the basketball game.

Grammar

Stage ❶ Get ready!

1 Read the chart. Look back at the article on page 20. Find examples of the past perfect.

> **Past perfect**
>
> - Finished past actions that occurred before another past action or time.
>   – Marta's mother **had** never **had** any experience helping a young soccer player.
>
>   **Remember!**
> - Past perfect actions occur *before* simple past actions.
>   – Marta arrived in Rio after she **had traveled** by bus for three days. (She traveled by bus. Then she arrived in Rio.)
> - We often use these time expressions with the past perfect, to indicate sequence of events.
>   *by the time / by + o'clock / by + month, year, before, after, when, as soon as, until …*
>
>   Language reference page 68

Stage ❷ Practice

2 Write affirmative and negative sentences and questions in the past perfect.

✓ by midnight / the / guests / leave
By midnight, the guests had left.

1 **?** he / play / soccer / before
_____

2 ✗ I / understand / the question
_____

3 ✓ Eliana / bring up / her children alone
_____

4 **?** where / they / leave / the keys
_____

5 ✗ we / travel / abroad / before
_____

6 ✓ by 2010 / Chen's talent / make / him / popular
_____

3 Complete the dialogue with the correct form of the verbs in parentheses. Use the past perfect.

Zoe What time did you get up yesterday, Max?
Max I got up at 5 a.m., although I (1) _____ (**not sleep**) well. I was so tired!
Zoe What did you do then?
Max After I (2) _____ (**eat**) breakfast, I went to the gym, and then the pool.
Zoe (3) _____ (**classes / start**) by the time you arrived at school?
Max No, I'm never late. But all my friends (4) _____ (**get**) there before me!
Zoe What happened after school?
Max After school (5) _____ (**finish**), I went to the pool again.
Zoe How long (6) _____ (**you / be**) in the pool when your mom arrived to take you home?
Max About two hours.
Zoe Did you relax at home?
Max Not really. After I (7) _____ (**do**) more exercises at home, I went to bed!

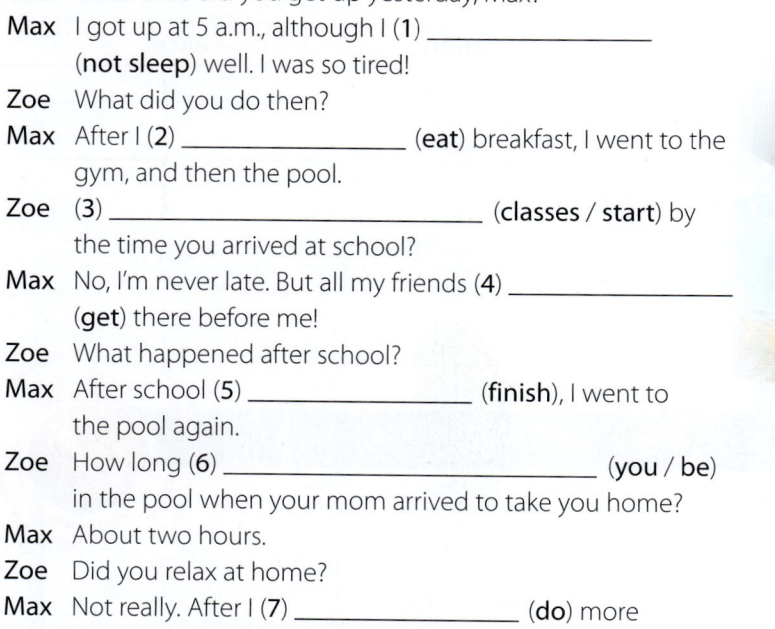

Sports Heroes 3

4 Circle the correct alternatives.
1. It was late when we **arrived** / **had arrived** home.
2. By 2008, the family **moved** / **had moved** to Sao Paulo.
3. When I **finished** / **had finished** my homework, I **had** / **had had** dinner.
4. We **couldn't go** / **hadn't gone** out until we **cleaned** / **had cleaned** our bedrooms.
5. Emma **walked** / **had walked** home after she **had been** / **went** swimming.
6. **Did you read** / **Had you read** the book before you **saw** / **had seen** the movie?

5 Complete the sentences. Use the past perfect and the simple past in each sentence.

By the time we _found_ (find) our seats, the game _had started_ (start).
1. Tom _____ (never visit) the stadium before he _____ (play) there.
2. I _____ (not call) my friends until I _____ (finish) my homework.
3. By the time the competition _____ (end), Eva _____ (win) three medals.
4. When we _____ (wash) the dishes, we _____ (sit) down to relax.
5. As soon as everyone _____ (arrive), the meeting _____ (begin).

6 Join the sentences. Write one verb in the past perfect and one in the simple past.

I saw the boots. Then I ordered them online.
As soon as _I had seen the boots, I ordered them online._

1. Her talent became obvious. Then she joined a team.
   By the time _____.
2. Ana and Ben were together for a year. Then they got married.
   Ana and Ben _____ before _____.
3. It stopped raining. Then I went for a run.
   When _____.
4. We went to the gym. Then we shared a pizza.
   After _____.

7 Read the blog. Complete it with the correct form of the verbs in parentheses. Use the past perfect or the simple past.

Brian's blog

As a teenager, I believed I was too cool for school. By ninth grade, I (1) _____ (be) in trouble too often. The principal expelled me when I (2) _____ (be) fifteen. That's when I (3) _____ (decide) I needed to change. Until I tried basketball at my new school, I (4) _____ (never want) to play sports – I had always thought I wasn't athletic enough. But as soon as I (5) _____ (catch) my first ball, I knew I (6) _____ (love) it. I worked hard to prove myself, and a few months later, (7) I _____ (become) a member of my high school team. By the end of my first season, I (8) _____ (play) in twenty games and I (9) _____ (score) a lot of points!

Grammar Get it right

Correct the errors in these sentences.

This unit
1. Our team had won the game last week.
2. When I arrived at school, I realized I'd forgot my homework.
3. The party hadn't started until everyone arrived.

Previous unit
4. Those soccer fans look sad. Their team should have lost.
5. You don't must go to the party if you don't want to.
6. I may to go to the gym tomorrow, but I'm not sure.

4 A Career in Music

Reading

Stage 1 Get ready!

1. Look at the photo. What do you think the woman does?
2. Skim the review and check your answer to exercise 1.
3. Find these words in the review. What do you think they mean?
   1. venue (n)   2. gig (n)   3. signed a deal (v)   4. cue (n)   5. tour (n)

HOME　NEWS　REVIEW　VI

HEADING FOR STARDOM
RUTH ROYALL
Under the Stars, Saturday November 12   Alison Sitwell

On a night when millions of British people are settling down to watch the TV singing competition *The X Factor*, you won't find me in front of the TV. I'm at Under the Stars, a small
5 venue in Bristol where a young woman named Ruth Royall is about to sing. You could compare Ruth with the singers on *The X Factor* who are competing for a career in the music industry. But unlike them, Ruth prefers to make her mark as a
10 musician without the help of TV talent shows.

Ruth is in her early twenties. She is a jazz and blues singer-songwriter who taught herself the piano and guitar. She has always wanted to be a professional musician. "I performed my first
15 solo gig at the age of 14," Ruth says, "in a bar whose customers were at least twice my age! But I loved it, and I haven't stopped performing since." Ruth's manager spotted her talent early on, and she signed a deal with a record company
20 when she was 18. "I never stop working on my writing, image, and sound," says Ruth. "I think they've improved a lot."

Wearing a cute red dress, with her guitarist, bassist, and drummer waiting for their cue, Ruth
25 smiles with confidence. She starts to sing, and her talent is obvious. Her voice reminds me of Ella Fitzgerald and Billie Holiday, the singing legends who are her greatest influences. "I really look up to them," Ruth says. She performs six
30 songs, but it is a beautiful song called *Mountains* which stands out the most. This is the song that she has just released on CD and as a download.

Ruth's life sounds glamorous and exciting, but behind the scenes, her schedule is
35 grueling. "I'm up at 5:30 every morning," she says, "and I work in a café until noon. I spend afternoons working as a singing tutor, something that I love doing. I also commute to the studio in Oxford where I rehearse." Some
40 weekends are spent rehearsing and recording, and gigs generally take place on weekends, too. There are also tours to fit in, and when she isn't doing all that, she's composing or practicing. There isn't much time to wind
45 down, but Ruth doesn't mind working hard.

When the gig is over, Ruth's enchanting voice still echoes in my ears. There's no magic to promote this girl to stardom. No TV show, no studio audience, no articles
50 in gossip magazines. Anyone who knows Ruth will agree that three things are helping her climb the ladder to success: talent, determination, and hard work.

Focus on false friends

4. Find these words in the text. Circle the correct definitions.
   1. confidence (line 25)   *certainty about your abilities and qualities / trust in someone*
   2. legends (line 28)   *subtitles or captions / very famous people*
   3. magazines (line 50)   *publications with articles and photos / department stores*

False friends list pages 60–61

A Career in Music 4

Stage 2 Read and understand

5 🔊 1.06 **Read the review again. Choose the correct answers.**

1 Under the Stars is …
   A a TV talent show.
   B the name of a song.
   C a place for musicians to perform.
   D a venue for talent competitions.
   E the name of Ruth Royall's band.

2 Ruth Royall …
   A can't play the guitar.
   B hasn't played the piano since she was fourteen.
   C is too young to be in a bar.
   D writes and sings her own songs.
   E has never performed alone.

3 Ruth …
   A isn't interested in her appearance.
   B isn't very confident.
   C is wearing red for her performance.
   D sings better than Ella Fitzgerald and Billie Holiday.
   E admires Billie Holiday's song, *Mountains*.

4 She …
   A starts her day very early.
   B lives in Oxford.
   C studies singing in the afternoon.
   D doesn't have time to go on tour.
   E never does gigs on weekends.

5 The writer says that Ruth …
   A doesn't stop singing when the gig finishes.
   B has never wanted to appear on TV.
   C doesn't buy gossip magazines.
   D doesn't mind climbing ladders.
   E is determined and gifted.

Reading strategy

Understanding pronouns
We use a variety of personal, possessive, and demonstrative pronouns and adjectives (for example: *it, them, their, that, these, the one(s)* …) to refer to things that we already mentioned. To understand these references:
1 Read the text. Underline the pronouns.
2 Read these parts of the text carefully. Match the pronouns with the nouns that they refer to.

6 Read the *Reading strategy* above. In the extracts from the review below, which nouns do the **bold** pronouns and possessive adjectives refer to?

… you won't find **me** in front of the TV. (line 3) _Alison Sitwell_

1 In a bar whose customers were probably at least twice **my** age! (line 15)
   _____

2 I think **they**'ve improved a lot. (line 21)
   _____

3 … her guitarist, bassist, and drummer waiting for **their** cue (line 23)
   _____

4 I really look up to **them** … (line 28)
   _____

Vocabulary

Verbs: music

1 Read the advertisements. Where can classical musicians take a course?

Flora Records is an Oregon-based record label. We're currently looking for unsigned folk musicians. We offer a modern studio where you can **practice** and **record** new tracks, and we'll help you **release** your music, too. We regularly **promote** our musicians on our website where fans can read blogs, find tour dates, and **download** music.

Would you like to have a career in music?

Do you dream of **composing** a symphony? Adams College is taking applications for its music courses. You'll **rehearse** for concerts with world-class musicians, write music with expert tutors, and **perform** at well-known venues.

Pick up a brochure to find out more.

2 Choose the correct answer for each sentence.

1. Jake has been ____ some new songs in the studio.
   A releasing   B recording   C promoting
2. My favorite band ____ their latest album last month.
   A released   B composed   C practiced
3. Ewan ____ the guitar for an hour every day.
   A rehearses   B composes   C practices
4. You can ____ Paula's new song from her website.
   A perform   B record   C download
5. The band is ____ for a concert next week.
   A recording   B promoting   C rehearsing

3 Complete the sentences with the correct noun forms of the verbs below.

compose • perform • promote • rehearse • release

1. That was an amazing _____. I never knew you could sing so well.
2. I love the great music legends, but I buy a lot of new _____ as well.
3. I missed so many _____, I couldn't take part in the concert.
4. Advertising concerts is part of record company _____.
5. I recognize the music, but I can't remember the name of the _____.

Focus on phrasal verbs

4 Write the infinitive form of the red phrasal verbs in these sentences. Match them with the definitions below.

admire • become calmer or quieter • be easily noticeable • relax after a period of stress or excitement

1. I love **winding down** at home after a long hard day.
2. Polly was the only girl in a red dress, so she really **stood out**.
3. Ben's much smarter than his sister. She has always **looked up to** him.
4. The kids were excited after the party, but they've **settled down** now.

Word list

compose
download
perform
practice
promote
record
rehearse
release

look up to
settle down
stand out
wind down

A Career in Music 4

Language workshop

Gerunds and infinitives (1)

- We put a gerund after some verbs (*enjoy*, *don't mind*, *can't stand* …)
  – Ruth doesn't mind **working** hard.
- We put *to* + infinitive after other verbs (*want*, *hope*, *need*, *would like* …)
  – Ruth has always wanted **to be** a professional musician.
- We can put a gerund OR *to* + infinitive after some verbs (*like*, *love*, *hate*, *prefer*).
  – She loves **to teach** singing. ✓
  – She loves **teaching** singing. ✓

Language reference page 71

5 Circle the correct alternatives.

I **enjoy** / **love** to sing.

1 Amy **likes** / **would like** being famous.
2 We **don't want** / **don't mind** to watch talent shows.
3 I **can't stand** / **hate** to go out in the rain.
4 Joe **needs** / **prefers** studying alone.
5 Maria **loves** / **hopes** performing her own songs.

Noun suffixes (2)

- To say what people's occupations are, we often use nouns ending in *-er*, *-ian*, *-ist*, or *-or*.
  – Ruth Royall is making her mark as a music**ian**.

Language reference page 71

6 Write the occupations based on these words. Use noun suffixes.

1 art — _artist_
2 science — _____
3 write — _____
4 act — _____
5 politics — _____
6 perform — _____
7 reception — _____
8 invent — _____
9 manage — _____
10 electric — _____
11 magic — _____
12 direct — _____

7 Complete the sentences with the correct occupations from exercise 6.

1 I had to call an _____ because all the lights had stopped working.
2 When I arrived at the hotel, the _____ gave me a key for my room.
3 An _____ comes up with ideas that no one has thought of before.
4 A _____ is a person who sings, dances, or tells jokes in front of an audience.
5 As a busy musician, I needed someone to organize my life, so I employed a _____ .
6 The _____ showed the children an empty hat, and then a rabbit jumped out of it!
7 I became a _____ because I'm very interested in what makes our world.
8 A _____ controls an activity, company, or part of a company.

Vocabulary Get it right

Correct the errors in these sentences.

This unit
1 Do you mind to wait outside?
2 Jenny hopes being famous one day.
3 The receptician spoke to the doctor for me.

Previous unit
4 Tom isn't enough good to play in a band.
5 I'm going to sign an agreement with an agent.
6 There's no differation between the two singers.

Grammar

Stage 1 Get ready!

1 Read the chart. Look carefully at the sentences. Which noun does each bold relative pronoun refer to?

Relative clauses (1)

- Defining relative clauses give essential information about things, people, possessions, places or times.
- We introduce defining relative clauses with relative pronouns: *that, which, who, whose, where,* or *when*.

that: things or people	– Working as a singing tutor is something **that** I love doing.
which: things	– *Mountains* is the song **which** stands out the most.
who: people	– Anyone **who** knows Ruth will agree that she works very hard.
whose: possession	– I performed in a bar **whose** customers were at least twice my age.
where: places	– I'm in a small venue **where** a young woman is about to sing.
when: times	– On a night **when** millions of people are watching TV …

Language reference page 70

Stage 2 Practice

2 Match sentence halves 1–6 with defining relative clauses A–F.

1 *Forever* is a song ____
2 Kelly is the girl ____
3 Paul is in a restaurant ____
4 I've just heard a young singer ____
5 It's the kind of evening ____
6 *The X Factor* is a TV talent show ____

A whose parents are both musicians.
B when most people prefer to stay inside.
C who might be perfect for your record company.
D which is very popular in the UK.
E that I wrote two years ago.
F where he's waiting for some friends.

3 Complete the sentences with *who, whose, where, when,* or *which*. Check (✓) the sentences where you can also use *that*.

1 ☐ This is the studio _____ we record new songs.
2 ☐ Sara was at an age _____ she wanted to leave home.
3 ☐ I'm wearing the shoes _____ I bought in Paris.
4 ☐ Paul Lopez is a young actor _____ is very popular in the US.
5 ☐ 1989 was the year _____ I first met your mother.
6 ☐ I'm talking to Tom Jackson _____ new album is now available.
7 ☐ My dad has an old cell phone _____ you can borrow.
8 ☐ I know a great café _____ we can have lunch.

A Career in Music 4

4 Read the *Language extra*. Cross out the relative pronouns that you can omit.

1 I prefer to listen to singers **who** write their own songs.
2 I hate listening to music **that** makes me sad.
3 The man **who** I spoke to told me the gig starts at half past eight.
4 I have a neighbor **whose** son is a well-known scientist.
5 This is the store **where** I bought my first CD.
6 I don't think you would enjoy the books **which** he reads.

> **Language extra**
> - We can omit the relative pronouns *that*, *which*, *who*, or *when* if they come before a noun or a pronoun.
>   – The song (that) she recently released.
> - We can never omit *whose* or *where*.
>
> **Remember!**
> *whose* = a relative pronoun for possession
> *who's* = who + is

5 Read the *Language extra* again. Complete the sentences with *who's* or *whose*.

1 Jack has a friend _____ bedroom is full of Rihanna posters.
2 I've just met the band _____ album I bought last week.
3 Have you spoken to anyone _____ going to the concert tonight?
4 That's the competitor _____ going to win.
5 _____ bag is this? I found it in the kitchen.
6 We went to watch my actor friend _____ in a play.

6 Find one error in each sentence and correct it.

Yuki is the boy (lives) next door. _who lives_

1 That's the restaurant when we ate last week. _____
2 Roberta has a singing tutor which has helped her a lot. _____
3 Ed is a young musician whose making his mark on the London music scene. _____
4 This is the studio that we rehearse and practice. _____
5 2009 was the year which I went to my first gig. _____
6 Two people took some items whose didn't belong to them. _____

7 Join the sentences with an appropriate relative pronoun.

I met a man. He works for a record company.
I met a man who works for a record company.

1 This is a café. I often go there on weekends.
_____

2 Anna has a friend. Her friend's house has ten bedrooms.
_____

3 Jared is a singer. He performs regularly at this venue.
_____

4 Linda likes reading science articles. They tell her about the universe.
_____

5 Carnival is a great time of year. We dress up and have fun.
_____

Grammar Get it right

Correct the errors in these sentences.

This unit
1 The woman which I told you about is sitting over there.
2 Whose going to the party tonight?
3 I'd like to see the house you were born.

Previous unit
4 I couldn't relax until I finished my homework.
5 By the time we had arrived, the gig nearly finished.
6 By 2010, they got married.

5 Different Worlds

Reading

Stage 1 Get ready!

1. Look at the photos. Where do you think the people are?
2. Skim the magazine article and check your answer to exercise 1.
3. Find these words in the article. What do you think they mean?
   1. devout *(adj)*   2. strict *(adj)*   3. squarest *(adj)*   4. illuminating *(adj)*

A period of freedom

1 In today's world, where electronic gadgets, fashion, and pop music are a normal part of life, it's hard to imagine teenagers living without them. Yet this is exactly what Amish teenagers have to do. The Bible guides the lives of the Amish, who are a devout Christian community that live mostly in the American Midwest. They worship regularly, observe a strict dress code, and use little electricity. Many abstain from drinking alcohol, too. They are a self-sufficient community who rarely leave their villages and whose children receive only a basic education. Because of all this, they have little knowledge of the outside world.

2 Channel 4, which is a British TV station, recently made a documentary called *Amish: World's Squarest Teenagers* in order to explore the differences between the Amish and modern British teenagers. In the show, Amish teens Leah Miller, her brother Andrew, and their friends Becky, Leon, and Jerry go to the UK. They spend a month there, trying out things which their community doesn't normally allow, and interacting with young British people.

3 The documentary follows the five friends during a special period in their lives called *Rumspringa*. This period, when Amish teenagers are allowed to have more freedom, begins around the age of 16. *Rumspringa*, which means "running around", allows Amish teenagers to experience things which are normally forbidden, such as drinking alcohol, dancing, wearing Western clothes, and living away from their parents. *Rumspringa* lasts several years, and ends when the young people choose to be baptized into the Amish church and to resume a stricter way of life.

4 During their month in the UK, the Amish teens come across many new situations. They are shocked to learn about street crime when they meet a mother whose son was stabbed and killed. They also struggle to accept the concepts of divorce and unmarried couples who live together. And visiting a nightclub, where the Amish teens are put off by the crowds and loud music, is also an illuminating experience!

5 But there are many positive experiences. In London, Jerry and a young British Muslim, who wants to follow a more religious lifestyle, discuss their beliefs and find common ground. In Cornwall, the Amish teens enjoy sharing their culture by building a wooden house for their hosts' chickens. And while traveling to the coast, Becky and Leah, who have never been to a beach before, wonder what color the ocean will be.

6 Although the beliefs of the Amish teenagers sometimes seem extreme, their visit has positive effects on the British teens. It brings up questions that make them reconsider their lives. The Amish teens' lives are so different, yet in many ways they seem happier and more peaceful than the young British people. And the Amish teens? After returning from the UK, the Amish are happy to be home again, but they have also learned from the experience. They now know that life may have more to offer than they had originally thought.

Focus on false friends

4. Find these words in the text. Circle the correct definitions.
   1. parents (line 28)   *mother and father / family members*
   2. resume (line 30)   *summarize something / begin something again*
   3. discuss (line 41)   *talk about something / argue about something*

False friends list pages 60–61

Different Worlds 5

Stage ❷ Read and understand

> **Reading strategy**
>
> **Using paragraph subheadings**
> 1 Paragraph subheadings give the main idea of the paragraph. As you read, underline the most important information in each paragraph.
> 2 When you have read each paragraph, think of your own subheading for it.

5 Read the *Reading strategy* above. Match subheadings A–F with paragraphs 1–6 from the article.

- A Culture shock   ____
- B The Amish on TV   ____
- C Positive aspects   ____
- D A simple lifestyle   ____
- E The results   ____
- F Time to experience different things ____

6 🔊 1.07 Read the article again. Choose the correct answers.

1 The five Amish teenagers …
  - A have spent their whole lives in the UK.
  - B travel to the UK for a month.
  - C can't go to the UK.
  - D buy their clothes from the UK.
  - E have never heard of the UK.

2 *Rumspringa* is a time when Amish teenagers …
  - A return to their community.
  - B leave the Amish church.
  - C can have greater freedom.
  - D must run around.
  - E must wear Western clothes.

3 The Amish teenagers …
  - A love everything about the UK.
  - B find that life in the UK is similar to their own.
  - C aren't surprised by street crime and divorce.
  - D dislike some aspects of British life.
  - E love the crowds and loud music.

4 During their stay …
  - A Jerry decides to change his lifestyle.
  - B the group builds a new home for their hosts.
  - C the girls visit the coast for the first time.
  - D the girls aren't interested in seeing the ocean.
  - E the group refuses to eat chicken.

5 At the end of the month …
  - A nothing is different.
  - B Becky and Leah have stopped wearing Amish clothes.
  - C the group doesn't want to go home.
  - D everyone has changed a little.
  - E the British teenagers quickly forget their Amish visitors.

7 Match definitions 1–5 with words or phrases in the article.

1 rules about what clothes people should wear (paragraph 1)
_____

2 able to do or produce everything without the help of other people (paragraph 1)
_____

3 not permitted (paragraph 3) _____

4 attacked with a knife (paragraph 4) _____

5 agree on something (paragraph 5) _____

33

Vocabulary

Verbs: lifestyle choices

1 Read the comments. Who would like to learn more about the Amish? Who doesn't know if they could live like the Amish?

Lily November 11
It must be hard for the Amish teenagers to <u>observe</u> so many rules every day. And I was surprised that their parents **allowed** them to travel to the UK!

Amir November 19
In the show, the teenagers learn that there are similarities between Muslims and Christians, although they <u>follow</u> different religions and <u>worship</u> in different ways.

Jake November 22
Traveling around the world I've <u>experienced</u> many different cultures, but the Amish are especially interesting. I'd love to **explore** their lifestyle further.

Gisela November 30
When you have a religion to **guide** you, I think it makes life easier. But could I **abstain** from 21st-century life like the Amish? I'm not sure.

2 Match the **bold** words in exercise 1 with definitions 1–4 below.
  1 decide not to do something you normally enjoy doing _____
  2 find out more information about something _____
  3 permitted to do or have something _____
  4 influence someone's actions and decisions _____

3 Look at the <u>underlined</u> words in exercise 1. Circle the correct alternatives.
  1 The Amish often **follow** / **worship** in their own homes.
  2 As children, we had to **experience** / **observe** our parents' rules.
  3 During *Rumspringa*, Amish teenagers **experience** / **worship** many new things.
  4 Amish children are willing to **worship** / **follow** older people's advice.

Focus on phrasal verbs

4 Write the infinitive form of the red phrasal verbs in these sentences. Match them with the definitions below.

> raise a topic to think about •
> cause someone to lose interest or enthusiasm •
> test something • find someone or something by chance

  1 Mom **tried out** the local food, but she wasn't impressed.
  2 Watching the documentary **brought up** a lot of discussion.
  3 I **came across** some old pictures while I was cleaning my room.
  4 Tom wanted to buy the sneakers, but the price **put** him **off**.

Word list
abstain
allow
experience
explore
follow
guide
observe
worship

bring up
come across
put off
try out

Different Worlds 5

Language workshop

Gerunds and infinitives (2)

We often use a gerund …
- as the subject or object of a sentence.
  – **Visiting a nightclub** is an eye-opening experience.
- after prepositions.
  – **After returning** from the UK, the Amish are happy to be home again.
- after some verbs (*enjoy, feel like, finish, don't mind, suggest* …).
  – The British teenagers enjoyed **meeting** their Amish counterparts.

We often use *to* + infinitive …
- to express purpose.
  – Many Amish choose **to join** the Amish church after *Rumspringa*.
- after adjectives.
  – It's hard **to imagine** teenagers living without pop music and fashion.
- after some verbs (*ask, help, need, seem, want* …).
  – Perhaps teenagers need **to experience** new things!

Language reference page 73

5 Complete the sentences with the correct form of the bold verbs. Use a gerund or *to* + infinitive.

1 The Amish go to the UK _____ their lives with those of British teenagers. (**compare**)
2 _____ time in another country can teach a person a lot. (**spend**)
3 My sister is always happy _____ her skills and ideas. (**share**)
4 I really want _____ abroad. (**travel**)
5 By _____ a simple life, the Amish feel close to their religion. (**live**)
6 A lot of viewers have enjoyed _____ the documentary. (**watch**)

Prefixes

Prefix	Meaning	Example
re-	again	reconsider
mis-	wrong	misunderstanding
over-	too much	overcrowding
non-	not	non-conformist

Prefix	Meaning	Example
self-	for, of, to, or by yourself	self-sufficient
inter-	between	interact

Language reference page 73

6 Complete the sentences with the correct prefixes from the chart above. Use a dictionary to help you.

We don't allow cigarettes in here. This is a _non_-smoking restaurant.

1 The competition is _____national. Teams from many countries are taking part.
2 Training for a marathon is hard. You need to be _____-disciplined.
3 Pablo doesn't like it when they _____make movies. He prefers the originals.
4 I shouldn't have gotten so angry. I know I _____reacted.
5 Sorry, I thought you said something different. I must have _____heard you.
6 The restaurant _____charged me. They must have made a mistake.

Vocabulary   Get it right

Correct the errors in these sentences.

This unit
1 Older people can experience you when you are making a difficult decision.
2 Before to leave, please turn off the lights.
3 All my money is gone. I think I must have respent this weekend.

Previous unit
4 "Did you compete that song?"
  "Yes, I wrote it myself."
5 I can't stand to watch documentaries!
6 He's a great performist – the crowd loved him.

35

Grammar

Stage 1 Get ready!

1 Read the chart. Look back at the text on page 32. <u>Underline</u> the relative clauses. Are they defining or non-defining? How do you know?

Relative clauses (2)

Defining relative clauses
- They give essential information about things, people, possessions, places, or times.
  - A community **that** live in the American Midwest.
  - That's the house **(which)** we bought last month.

  In these clauses,
  - we can omit the relative pronouns *that*, *which*, *who*, or *when*, if they come before a noun or a pronoun.
  - we can't omit *whose* or *where*.

Non-defining relative clauses
- They give extra information about things, people, possessions, places, or times.
  - *Rumspringa*, **which** means "running around", allows Amish teenagers …

  In these clauses,
  - we must use commas to separate the clause from the rest of the sentence.
  - we can't omit any relative pronoun.
  - we can't use the relative pronoun *that*.

Remember!
- We introduce relative clauses with relative pronouns (*that*, *which*, *who*, *whose*, *where*, *when*).
- A relative clause gives information about the noun that comes before it.
  - Channel 4, **which is a British TV station**, recently made a documentary. (noun = *Channel 4*; information = *it is a British TV station*.)

Language reference page 72

Stage 2 Practice

2 Circle the correct alternatives. Which sentences contain defining relative clauses (*D*) and which contain non-defining (*ND*)?

The Amish people, which / (who) originally came from Switzerland, speak a language called "Pennsylvania Dutch". _ND_

1 This is the documentary **that** / **who** I've been telling you about. ____
2 Leah, **whose** / **who** brother is also in the group, is happy to return home. ____
3 Ohio, **that** / **which** is a state in the US, is home to many Amish people. ____
4 Tourists **who** / **whose** travel to Ohio can visit the Amish villages. ____
5 The 18th century was the time **which** / **when** many Amish moved to North America. ____

3 Complete the non-defining relative clauses with the relative pronouns below.

when • where • which • who • whose

1 Pennsylvania Dutch, _____ is the Amish community's language, is similar to German.
2 During *Rumspringa*, _____ teenagers have more freedom, normal rules don't apply.
3 Becky and Leah, _____ dresses are homemade, don't feel comfortable in Western clothes.
4 Leah's home, _____ she lives with her family, doesn't have many electronic gadgets.
5 The British teenagers, _____ live in different parts of the UK, share their lives with the Amish.

Different Worlds 5

4 Read the text. Use the sentences below to complete the text with non-defining relative clauses. Be careful to use the correct relative pronouns.

> The sun disappears for months. • It is their traditional way of finding food. • It is called "Inuktun". • It contains a lot of meat. • He is a researcher at Cambridge University.

In 2010, Dr. Stephen Pax Leonard, (1) _____, spent a year living with the Inugguit people in northwest Greenland. The region, (2) _____, taught him about the difficulties some people face to protect their unique culture. Traveling on ice to hunt animals, (3) _____, is now very dangerous because of global warming. The typical Inugguit diet, (4) _____, is high in fat and contains few vegetables. And their language, (5) _____, is also in danger because they rarely write it down.

5 Join the sentences with defining relative clauses. If you can omit the relative pronoun, put it in parentheses.

Christopher Columbus was an explorer. He discovered the Americas.
Christopher Columbus was an explorer who discovered the Americas.

1 Alberto has a new girlfriend. Her parents are Swiss.
   Alberto _____.
2 Inuktun is a language. Some people in Greenland speak it.
   Inuktun _____.
3 I recently met a scientist. She spent several months in Antarctica.
   I _____.
4 The UK is a country. People from many different cultures live there.
   The UK _____.
5 My cousin is married to a man. I knew him at school.
   My cousin _____.
6 Greenland is a large island. It is part of Denmark.
   Greenland _____.

6 Add commas to these sentences where necessary. Can you omit any relative pronouns?

My brother, who lives in Porto Alegre, is a Spanish teacher.

1 Tourists who visit Yosemite National Park can explore its natural beauty.
2 My friend Jack who doesn't have a TV spends a lot of time reading books.
3 This is the church where my parents worship.
4 The clothes that I wear are very different from my brother's.
5 In the summer when it gets warm we often go to the beach.

Grammar   Get it right

Correct the errors in these sentences.

This unit
1 Mrs. Lewis, that lives next door, used to work as a journalist.
2 Andrew who has never traveled before is planning a trip to Europe.
3 People which watch the show will find the Amish lifestyle surprising.

Previous unit
4 Christopher Columbus was an explorer which family came from Italy.
5 This is the studio we recorded our last album.
6 The 1980s was a time that MP3 players didn't exist.

37

6 TV Trends

Reading

Stage 1 Get ready!

1. Read the title and skim the essay. Is the essay for or against reality TV, or neutral?
2. Read the essay and check your answer to exercise 1.
3. Scan the essay. What do the following figures refer to?
   1. 1999   2. 58%   3. 2002–7   4. 9%

CULTURE | HISTORY | SC

CULTURE
Is reality TV worth watching?

1 In 1999, nine Dutch strangers were locked inside the first ever *Big Brother* house. Since then, TV stations around the world have broadcast a steady stream of reality shows, including weight-loss competitions, celebrities showing off their amazing lifestyles, and contestants surviving on desert islands. Whereas the shows have many different formats, they share one focus: the behavior of their cast members.

2 Fans of reality shows are intrigued and often moved by the cast members' behavior as they laugh, cry, fall out, or fall in love. Their actions are discussed on Twitter and Facebook, and fans can keep up with the latest episodes online. Between 2002 and 2011, reality shows were watched by, on average, 58% of US primetime audiences. The ongoing popularity of these shows means that new formats are constantly being developed. However, reality show producers are regularly accused of making up storylines and portraying cast members in deliberately positive or negative ways to keep viewers interested. Critics also complain about the lack of serious content and the possible harmful effects of the genre.

3 In *Extreme Makeover*, which was shown in the US between 2002 and 2007, women had cosmetic surgery done because they felt unattractive. Some critics felt this gave viewers the wrong message: that you must be good-looking in order to be happy. And *Real Housewives*, a show where wealthy women are filmed in exclusive locations wearing designer clothes or having beauty treatments done, was felt by some to give unrealistic expectations to impressionable viewers.

4 In contrast, reality TV can raise awareness of controversial topics and has been praised for its ability to reduce racist attitudes. With cast members often from a range of ethnic groups, viewers begin to disregard ethnic backgrounds as they learn more about the people on the show. In international editions of *Big Brother*, topics such as racism, alcohol abuse, and disability are sometimes discussed by the housemates, which can lead to a better understanding of these issues. Furthermore, some reality shows can be educational. *Teen Mom*, in which teenage mothers struggle with parenthood, may have taught viewers a valuable lesson: teen pregnancies in the US fell by 9% while the first two seasons were being shown.

5 On the one hand, it's understandable that some people think reality TV is boring and not worth watching. Reality shows are often criticized for not having any genuinely entertaining or educational content. On the other hand, some reality shows are better than others. We may not always approve of the behavior of the cast members, but we might learn something from them about the world we live in.

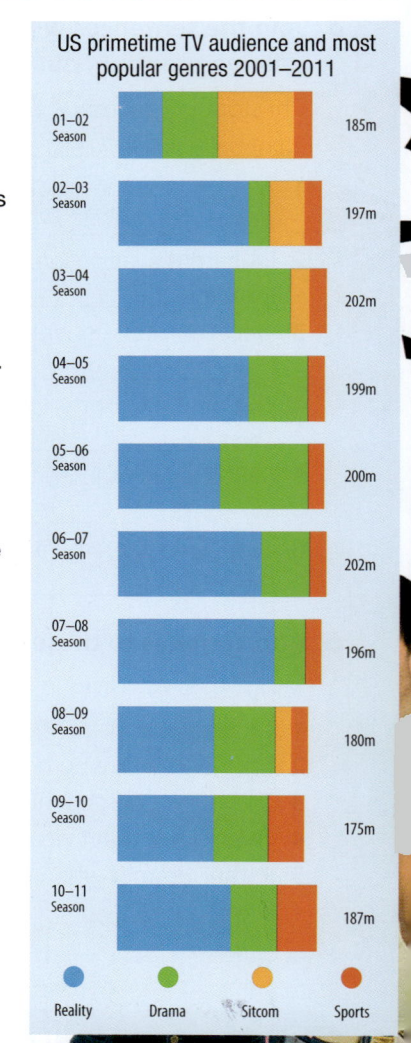

US primetime TV audience and most popular genres 2001–2011

Season	Viewers
01–02	185m
02–03	197m
03–04	202m
04–05	199m
05–06	200m
06–07	202m
07–08	196m
08–09	180m
09–10	175m
10–11	187m

● Reality ● Drama ● Sitcom ● Sports

Focus on false friends

4. Find these words in the text. Circle the correct definitions.

   1. strangers (line 1)   people from another country / people that you don't know
   2. locations (line 39)   places where a movie or TV show is filmed / leases or rentals
   3. topics (line 44)   subjects that people talk about / most important points

False friends list pages 60–61

TV Trends 6

Stage 2 Read and understand

Reading strategy

Making inferences
1 Read the text carefully. Sometimes you need to interpret the text to answer a question.
2 Look for clues in the text, such as the tone of the comments and the examples the writer uses.

5 Read the *Reading strategy* above. Follow steps 1 and 2. The writer thinks …

A reality TV shows are boring.
B the popularity of reality TV is decreasing.
C reality TV can make people more tolerant.
D *Teen Mom* makes parenting look easy.
E participants on reality TV shows teach us nothing.

6 🔊 1.08 Read the essay again. Choose the correct answers.

1 Since 1999 …
  A *Big Brother* has been the most popular show on TV.
  B celebrities' lifestyles have become more amazing.
  C there have been many reality shows on TV.
  D some celebrities have lived on a desert island.
  E people's behavior on reality shows has gotten worse.

2 TV viewers …
  A aren't very interested in reality shows.
  B often discuss reality shows online.
  C find fans of reality shows intriguing.
  D prefer to watch reality shows online.
  E often complain about reality shows.

3 In the US …
  A TV stations rarely introduce new reality shows.
  B everyone wants to wear designer clothes.
  C most women want to have cosmetic surgery.
  D reality shows don't always give the right message.
  E reality shows feature invented characters.

4 Reality TV …
  A can draw attention to controversial issues.
  B should show more people from different ethnic backgrounds.
  C avoids bringing up subjects that are difficult to talk about.
  D discourages teenagers from taking responsibility.
  E has increased the number of teenage pregnancies.

5 According to the graph, US TV viewing figures show that …
  A drama shows were the most popular show in 2005–6.
  B sitcoms have always been popular.
  C more people watch sports than drama.
  D sports shows were the least popular in 2008–9.
  E reality shows in 2007–8 were especially popular.

7 Find these words in the essay. What do you think they mean?

1 primetime (paragraph 2) _____
2 ongoing (paragraph 2) _____
3 impressionable (paragraph 3) _____
4 praised (paragraph 4) _____
5 disregard (paragraph 4) _____

Vocabulary

Television

1 Read the online web chat about the reality show, *The Streets*. Where do they make the show?

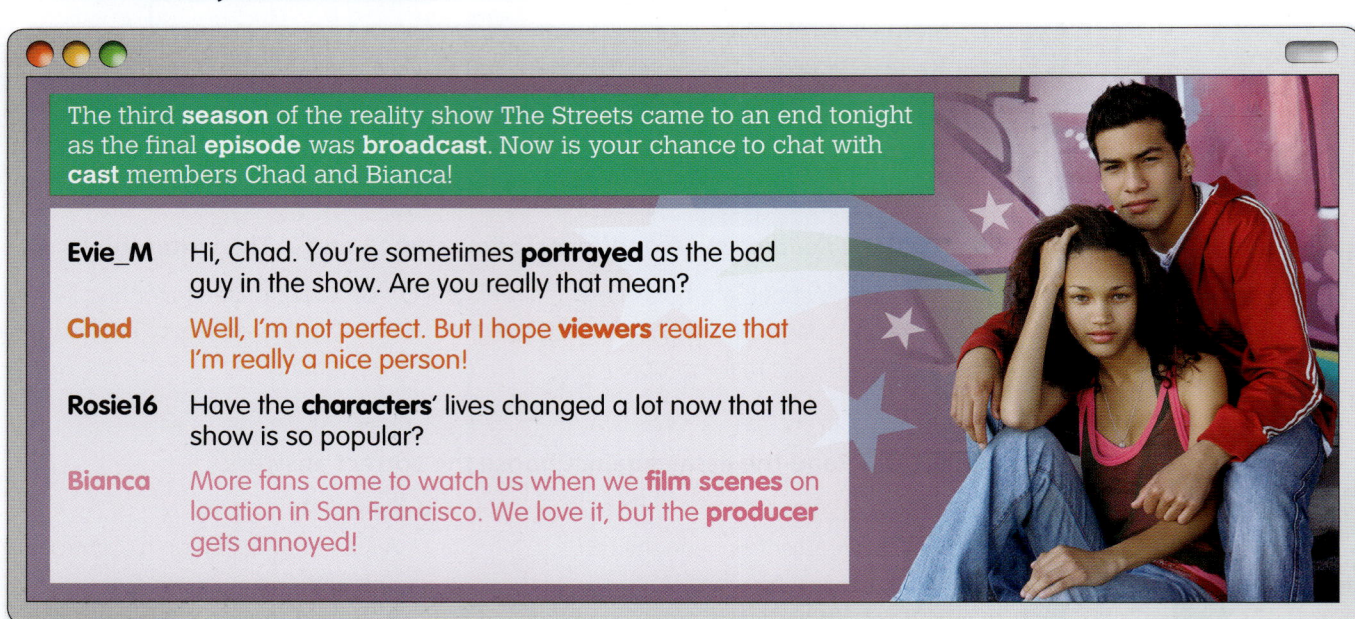

The third **season** of the reality show The Streets came to an end tonight as the final **episode** was **broadcast**. Now is your chance to chat with **cast** members Chad and Bianca!

Evie_M Hi, Chad. You're sometimes **portrayed** as the bad guy in the show. Are you really that mean?

Chad Well, I'm not perfect. But I hope **viewers** realize that I'm really a nice person!

Rosie16 Have the **characters**' lives changed a lot now that the show is so popular?

Bianca More fans come to watch us when we **film scenes** on location in San Francisco. We love it, but the **producer** gets annoyed!

2 Match the **bold** words in exercise 1 with definitions 1–10 below.

1 people who watch a TV show _____
2 person in charge of the financial aspects of making a TV show or movie _____
3 group of actors in a TV show, play, or movie _____
4 one section of a story on TV or radio that is in several parts _____
5 record a movie or a show on camera _____
6 people in a TV show, movie, book, or play _____
7 transmitted (of TV or radio shows) _____
8 a series of TV shows in a period of time _____
9 described in a particular way _____
10 parts of a show or movie where the action happens in one place _____

Focus on phrasal verbs

3 Write the infinitive form of the red phrasal verbs in these sentences. Match them with definitions below.

- learn about or be aware of news or current events
- try to impress others by talking about your abilities, etc.
- invent a story
- have a disagreement with someone so that you are no longer friends

1 My brothers have **fallen out** with each other. They aren't speaking to each other.
2 Amelia is **showing off** about her movie award again. I'm not interested!
3 Since Katy moved to France, we've **kept up with** each other through Facebook.
4 Tom said he dated a reality TV star, but he didn't really. He **made** it **up**.

Word list
broadcast
cast
character
episode
film
portray
producer
scene
season
viewer

fall out
keep up with
make up
show off

TV Trends 6

Language workshop

-ed and -ing adjectives

- We can make adjectives by adding -ed or -ing to some verbs.
  Language reference page 75

4 Look at the **bold** adjectives in sentences 1 and 2. Match them with explanations A and B below.

1 The show is **interesting**. ____   2 I'm **interested** in the show. ____
A This adjective describes how a person is feeling.
B This adjective describes the thing or situation that produces the feeling.

5 Circle the correct alternatives.

1 We're so **bored** / **boring**. There isn't anything to do.
2 The ending to the play was **intriguing** / **intrigued**. I didn't really understand it.
3 My brother was **disappointing** / **disappointed** not to win the competition.
4 The movie *Titanic* is very **moved** / **moving**. You can't watch it without crying!
5 I was **amazed** / **amazing** when I saw Zack on TV.

have / get something done

- *have* or *get* (any tense) + object + past participle
  – We use *have / get something done* to talk about things that are done for us by other people, usually professionals.
  Language reference page 75

6 Reorder the words to make sentences with *have / get something done*.

always / done / I / have / my make-up *I always have my make-up done.*

1 Ella / her own storyline / is / written / having
   _____

2 had / our costumes / We / made
   _____

3 were / The actors / their hair / having / styled
   _____

7 Rewrite the sentences with *have / get something done*. Use the correct tense.

Someone buys my clothes for me.   I *have my clothes bought for me.*

1 Someone prepares the actors' meals.
   The actors _____.
2 Someone is decorating Ben's house.
   Ben _____.
3 Someone took Demi Lovato's photo.
   Demi Lovato _____.
4 Someone cleans our car every week.
   We _____.

Vocabulary   Get it right

Correct the errors in these sentences.

This unit
1 Some actors are filmed as horrible people.
2 Everyone was intriguing by the story.
3 Lydia is having her hair did. The party is this evening.

Previous unit
4 Your friends can observe you when you aren't sure what to do.
5 After watch the show, Jessica went to bed.
6 I've misconsidered my opinions about reality TV.

41

Grammar

Stage 1 Get ready!

1 Read the chart. Look back at the text on page 38. <u>Underline</u> the passive sentences. What tenses are they?

The passive (1)

- We use the passive when the person who does the action is unknown, obvious, or less important than the action.
- The object in the active sentence becomes the subject in the passive sentence.
- We form the passive with *be* + past participle.

Note the tenses and the object–subject movement in these sentences:

	Active	Passive
Simple present	They accuse **producers** of making up storylines.	→ **Producers** are accused of making up storylines.
Simple past	They locked **nine Dutch strangers** inside the *Big Brother* house.	→ **Nine Dutch strangers** were locked inside the *Big Brother* house.
Present continuous	They are constantly developing **new formats**.	→ **New formats** are constantly being developed.
Past continuous	They were filming **the cast members**.	→ **The cast members** were being filmed.

Language reference page 74

Stage 2 Practice

2 Circle the correct active or passive alternatives.

1 Reality shows **sometimes think** / **are sometimes thought** to be educational.
2 Some teenagers **spend** / **are spent** many hours in front of a TV or computer.
3 I **was told** / **told** about the series by a friend.
4 The series ended because it was **losing** / **being lost** viewers.
5 Last night I **met** / **was met** some of the cast from my favorite reality show.
6 The DVD **sells** / **is sold** in stores and online.

3 Read the active sentences and complete the passive ones.

They discuss different topics. Different topics _are discussed_.

1 They didn't allow me to see the movie. I _____ allowed to see the movie.
2 They are filming the shows in my town. The shows _____ filmed in my town.
3 They told her she could join the cast. She _____ she could join the cast.
4 They were making the show this week. The show was _____ this week.

4 Circle the objects in these active sentences. Rewrite them as passive sentences.

A journalist is interviewing (the cast) for a gossip magazine.
The cast is being interviewed by a journalist for a gossip magazine.

1 They ask the producer a lot of questions.
_____

2 They are writing new storylines at the moment.
_____

3 They sent Amy home from the competition.
_____

4 Some people were talking about Daniel.
_____

TV Trends 6

5 Read the *Language extra*. Reorder the words to make passive questions.

the show / filmed / Where / was ? _Where was the show filmed?_

1 is / sent / home / Who / tonight / being ?
_____

2 made / the show / How / is ?
_____

3 you / about the decision / When / told / were ?
_____

> **Language extra**
> **Passive questions**
> - In passive questions, the subject goes immediately after the first verb in the sentence.
>   – How do they do **this**?
>   ➡ How is **this** done?
>   – Were they making up **the storylines**?
>   ➡ Were **the storylines** being made up?

6 Rewrite the active questions as passive questions.

Are they choosing the participants today?
Are the participants being chosen today?

1 Where did they film *Extreme Makeover*?
_____

2 Do they broadcast the show in the evenings?
_____

3 Was someone telling you what to say?
_____

4 Is someone repairing your TV set?
_____

7 Complete the text with the verbs below. Use the correct active or passive forms.

broadcast • film • make • hear • portray • take • use • watch

The sitcom *I Love Lucy* (1) _____ in the 1950s following a style that many sitcoms still (2) _____ today. The show (3) _____ from a studio with a live audience. You could often (4) _____ the audience laugh while the scenes (5) _____ .

Most of the sitcom (6) _____ place in a few rooms of an apartment, and the characters were very amusing. Over fifty years later, the show is still very popular, but why (7) _____ it _____ by 40 million Americans each year? Perhaps it's the show's simplicity that attracts viewers – or the way the characters (8) _____, which reminds us of ourselves. Whatever the reason, *I Love Lucy* is one example of the genre's enduring popularity.

Grammar Get it right

Correct the errors in these sentences.

This unit
1 Actors don't used in reality shows.
2 Tonight three people were send home from the competition.
3 When the movie was made?

Previous unit
4 The housemate, who I like most, left this week.
5 *Big Brother*, was first shown in 1999, is still popular today.
6 I have a DVD, you can borrow.

43

7 Protecting Our Planet

Reading

Stage 1 Get ready!

1 Look at the title of the infographic. What do we use oil for in our everyday lives?

2 Find these words in the text. What do you think they mean?

1 fossil fuel (n)   3 waste (n)   5 carbon emissions (n)
2 wind turbine (n) 4 congestion (n) 6 locally-sourced (adj)

Transition to a world without oil

A Oil is a precious commodity. Over the last 150 years, this fossil fuel has been used in many ways: powering ⁵vehicles, heating buildings, and manufacturing products. It has improved our lives immeasurably. But our supply is being depleted. ¹⁰Despite recent oil discoveries, it is anticipated that one day it will be used up.

B Although the planet has vast reserves of ¹⁵other fossil fuels, such as coal, tar sands, and natural gas, many people disagree with their use because they ²⁰are expensive to extract and they pollute the environment.

C In 2005, the Transition Movement was founded in Ireland. The movement consists of a network of "Transition communities" (ordinary neighborhoods, ²⁵villages, and towns) that use "green" and sustainable methods for energy, transportation, construction, and food. These communities believe that neither oil nor other fossil fuels are indispensable to modern standards of living: we simply need to rethink the way we use and produce our ³⁰energy. By 2010, more than 400 Transition communities had been set up around the world, and the movement is still growing. So what does the Transition Movement think ³⁵we should do?

D Energy: Wind turbines and solar panels can be installed to provide local areas with renewable energy. Waste can also be recycled to ⁴⁰generate heat and electricity. It is hoped that by 2025, 25% of the US's energy will be supplied by these and other renewable energy sources. This means that fuel consumption ⁴⁵can be reduced.

E Transportation: Phasing out cars in city centers and introducing more public transportation could reduce congestion and cut carbon emissions ⁵⁰by around 50% per passenger mile. More electric cars and bike paths would also cut down on air and noise pollution. As a result, our towns and cities would be cleaner, quieter, ⁵⁵and safer.

F Construction: Locally-sourced materials such as wood and bricks should be used for construction. Consequently, less fuel would be ⁶⁰required to transport materials. Homes should be well insulated so that less energy is needed for heating. And installing energy monitors would measure electricity use and help ⁶⁵reduce bills.

G Food: Food should be grown locally. Fruit and nut trees and vegetables could be planted on communal land, which would be allocated by local ⁷⁰councils. Since communities would be more self-sufficient, they would need to buy fewer groceries from the store. Therefore, less food would be imported by air and less fuel would ⁷⁵be used for transportation.

Focus on false friends

3 Find these words in the text. Circle the correct definitions.

1 anticipated (line 11) *expected / did something early*
2 vegetables (line 67) *a plant eaten as food / anything grown in the ground*
3 groceries (line 72) *rudeness / food and other goods from a supermarket*

False friends list pages 60–61

Protecting Our Planet   7

Stage 2 Read and understand

4 🔊 1.09 **Read the infographic again. Choose the correct answers.**

1 Oil …
   A was first discovered 150 years ago.
   B will soon be used up.
   C has been very important for transportation.
   D isn't very precious in our lives.
   E and other fossil fuels help protect the environment.

2 The Transition Movement believes we should …
   A use fossil fuels other than oil.
   B only use "green" forms of transportation.
   C change the way we use energy.
   D use more oil in our cooking.
   E grow more green plants.

3 Fuel consumption can be reduced by …
   A reducing waste.
   B using 25% less energy.
   C installing solar panels on cars.
   D using a variety of renewable energy sources.
   E providing more waste recycling centers.

4 According to the text, public transportation …
   A should be reduced by 50%.
   B produces a lot of carbon emissions.
   C has too many passengers.
   D is safer than biking.
   E cuts down on road congestion.

5 It's a good idea to …
   A create energy from locally-sourced wood.
   B monitor electricity use in homes.
   C insulate transportation.
   D use locally-sourced materials as fuel.
   E import energy from other countries.

6 People in Transition communities should be able to …
   A insulate their own homes.
   B provide most of the food they need.
   C cut down on noise pollution.
   D plant only fruit and nuts.
   E take risks to protect the planet.

Reading strategy

Identifying synonyms and antonyms

1 Look at the word in the question. Is it a noun, verb, adjective, or adverb?
2 Read the paragraph. Underline the words of this type. Which of these is a synonym (a word with the **same** meaning) for the word in the question?
3 Replace this word with the word in the question. Does the text still make sense?
4 You may be asked to find an antonym – a word with the **opposite** meaning.

5 Read the *Reading strategy* above. Follow steps 1–4. Find synonyms in the infographic to match words 1–5 below. Then use your dictionary to find an antonym for each word.

1 store (*n*) (paragraph A)   synonym: _____
                                     antonym: _____

2 huge (*adj*) (paragraph B)   synonym: _____
                                     antonym: _____

3 vital (*adj*) (paragraph C)   synonym: _____
                                     antonym: _____

4 contemporary (*adj*) (paragraph C)   synonym: _____
                                        antonym: _____

5 public (*adj*) (paragraph G)   synonym: _____
                                     antonym: _____

H The decision is ours. We can resort to other fossil fuels or we can follow the Transition path. Either we risk running out of oil, or we take action now, and create a bright future for our planet.

Vocabulary

Verbs: environment

1 Read the Transition town meeting agenda. What are the group's main concerns?

Little Paso Transition Town
Town meeting agenda – July 8

1. Review the use of land allocated for growing communal food:
   - we are still **consuming** too much **imported** food
   - water supplies are being **depleted** too quickly by too many people watering their plants in the communal garden

   Suggested solution: council to **allocate** more land to **plant** more fruit trees and vegetables

2. Review energy efficiency in homes:
   - solar panels have been **installed** on more than 50 houses in the community to **generate** more energy, but energy bills are still high in some homes

   Suggested solution: **insulate** homes for free to help **reduce** fuel bills

3. Discuss any other business

2 Look at the **bold** verbs in exercise 1. Circle the correct alternatives.
1. Volunteers have **planted** / **depleted** several trees in the communal garden.
2. The train company plans to **import** / **install** free Wi-Fi for all its customers.
3. The wind turbine **generates** / **installs** enough energy to power 400 homes.
4. Why do we **import** / **generate** so much food from other countries?
5. Without sufficient food, the body's energy levels will be **consumed** / **depleted**.

3 Which **bold** verbs in the agenda can take the noun suffix *-ion*?

4 Complete the sentences with the noun forms of the verbs below.

allocate • consume • deplete • insulate • reduce

1. The house was very cold in winter without _____.
2. The council wants to discuss the land _____ for communal gardens.
3. The _____ of water supplies in rivers is caused by our need for fresh water.
4. The _____ of carbon emissions is an important goal for countries.
5. The Transition Movement encourages the reduced _____ of fossil fuels.

Focus on phrasal verbs

5 Write the infinitive form of the red phrasal verbs in these sentences. Match them with the definitions below.

- reduce the amount or number of something
- stop using something gradually in stages over a period of time
- use something because there is no better option
- use all of something so there is nothing left

1. We didn't open a new ketchup bottle until we'd **used up** the old one.
2. The old style dollar bills will be **phased out** next year.
3. Lizzie is **cutting down on** chocolate – she knows she eats too much!
4. Without a stove, we've **resorted to** eating takeout food every night.

Word list
allocate
consume
deplete
generate
import
install
insulate
plant
reduce

cut down on
phase out
resort to
use up

Protecting Our Planet 7

Language workshop

either ... or and neither ... nor

either ... or ...
- This shows a choice between two possibilities.
  – Carlos can meet us on Monday. He can meet us on Tuesday.
  – Carlos can meet us **either** on Monday **or** on Tuesday.

neither ... nor ...
- This joins two negative ideas. It is the opposite of *both ... and ...* . It is very formal.
  – Their ideas aren't good. Their ideas aren't interesting.
  – Their ideas are **neither** good **nor** interesting.

Language reference page 76

6 Rewrite the sentences with the **bold** words.

1 I'll bring a pizza to the party. I'll bring a salad to the party. (**either / or**)
   _____
2 We don't have solar panels. We don't have an energy monitor. (**neither / nor**)
   _____
3 Oil and coal aren't good for the environment. (**neither / nor**)
   _____
4 The meeting wasn't interesting or helpful. (**neither / nor**)
   _____

Prefixes and suffixes

Prefixes	dis-, im-, in-, ir-, mis-, over-, re-, self-, un-, under-
Noun suffixes	-ance, -ation, -ence, -er, -ian, -ion, -ist, -or, -ment
Adjective suffixes	-able, -al, -ful, -ic, -ish, -ive, -less, -ous, -y

Language reference page 77

7 Complete the sentences with a prefix from the chart above. Use a dictionary to help you.

1 Humans can't live without air. It's _____ possible.
2 The argument was due to a _____ understanding.
3 I learned to play the guitar without help. I'm _____-taught.
4 Grandma wants to _____ visit the town where she grew up.
5 You don't need so much food. It's _____ necessary.
6 We were late because we _____ estimated the time the journey would take.

8 Complete the sentences with a suffix from the chart above.

1 That's a great painting. You're very creat_____.
2 The solar panels were installed by a local build_____.
3 We need to be realist_____ about climate change.
4 It's self_____ not to protect the environment for the next generat_____.
5 Wind turbines may provide electricity, but they're not very attract_____.
6 Since Rob Hopkins began the Transition Move_____, he's become fam_____.

Vocabulary   Get it right

Correct the errors in these sentences.

This unit
1 Some people believe we should insulate our consumption of fossil fuels.
2 I can meet you either tomorrow nor Sunday.
3 With a little imaginion, the Transition Movement can succeed.

Previous unit
4 The first episode was cast on TV last night.
5 I was amazing when I heard the latest global warming figures.
6 We need to have an energy monitor install as soon as possible.

Grammar

Stage 1 Get ready!

1 Read the chart. Look back at the text on page 44. <u>Underline</u> the passive sentences. What tenses are they in?

The passive (2)

- In passive sentences, to say who or what does the action, we use *by* + agent.
  – The Transition Movement was founded **by Rob Hopkins**.
- We can omit *by* + agent if the person or thing who does the action is unknown, obvious, or less important than the action.

Remember!
- We use the passive voice when we want to emphasize what happens to people or things.
- We use the active voice when we want to emphasize what people or things do.

	Active	Passive
Present perfect	We **have used** oil in many ways.	→ Oil **has been used** in many ways.
Past perfect	By 2010, they **had set up** more than 400 Transition communities.	→ By 2010, more than 400 Transition communities **had been set up**.
will	We **will use up** oil.	→ Oil **will be used up**.
Modals	It **could reduce** energy bills.	→ Energy bills **could be reduced**.

Language reference page 76

Stage 2 Practice

2 Circle the correct active or passive alternatives.

1. We **have just bought / have just been bought** a new house.
2. Fossil fuels **shouldn't overuse / shouldn't be overused**.
3. By last year, 200 people **had joined / had been joined** the movement.
4. All our friends **will invite / will be invited** to the party.
5. Garden waste **can use / can be used** to generate electricity.
6. He **has done / has been done** research into solar energy.

3 Write passive sentences. Use the prompts and the tenses or modals in parentheses.

vegetables / plant (*could*) <u>Vegetables could be planted.</u>

1. climate change / prevent (*must*)
   _____

2. more energy / generate (**present perfect**)
   _____

3. nobody / tell (**past perfect**)
   _____

4. problems / cause (*will*)
   _____

5. your help / not need (*might*)
   _____

4 Read the sentences. Cross out *by* + agent where appropriate.

A meeting has been arranged ~~by us~~.

1. Breakfast will be served at eight thirty by waiters.
2. I was told about the Transition Movement by a friend.
3. All the materials had been delivered by the building company.
4. We were very impressed by Paul and Angela's new home.

Protecting Our Planet   7

5 Rewrite the active sentences as passive sentences. Omit *by* + agent where appropriate.

We sell *The Transition Handbook* here. *The Transition Handbook is sold here.*

1 I will send the invitations next week.
   _____.

2 By yesterday, a million people had watched the video.
   _____.

3 Rising fuel bills have caused problems.
   _____.

4 They can recycle waste to generate electricity.
   _____.

6 Put the words in order to write questions in the passive.

where / been / the new heating system / built / has ?
Where has the new heating system been built?

1 the car / be / can / repaired ?
   _____

2 the house / many people / has / seen / been / by ?
   _____

3 the books / in / sent / will / the mail / be ?
   _____

4 be / when / told / the residents / should ?
   _____

7 Read the text. Complete it with the correct active or passive form of the verbs in parentheses. Use the simple present, present perfect, past perfect, *will*, or a modal verb.

Electric cars first appeared in the nineteenth century, but their popularity (1) _____ (**increase**) significantly in recent years. The latest models (2) _____ (**design**) to offer significant advantages over gasoline-powered cars. They are quieter and cheaper to run, and they (3) _____ (**not pollute**) the environment. However, there are disadvantages, too. Electric cars are expensive, and (4) _____ (**can only drive**) short distances before their batteries run out. By the end of 2011, only a small number of electric cars (5) _____ (**sell**). However, as technology improves, their prices (6) _____ (**fall**). In the future, many more electric cars (7) _____ (**see**) on our streets.

Grammar   Get it right

Correct the errors in these sentences.

This unit
1 Three apartments have been bought by buyers.
2 We have been agreed to grow vegetables together.
3 In the future, less fossil fuel will used.

Previous unit
4 Solar panels can install in most homes.
5 I was tell about transition towns.
6 Where are being planted the crops?

49

8 Bad Behavior

Reading

Stage 1 Get ready!

1. Read the title. What do you think the new approach could be?
2. Skim the newspaper article and check your answers to exercise 1.
3. Find these words in the article. What do you think they mean?
   1. reoffend *(v)*   2. lenient *(adj)*   3. skipping school *(v)*

A new approach to youth crime

Despite the fact that sending youth offenders to prison makes them more likely to reoffend, the US has one of the world's highest rates of juvenile incarceration. Currently, there are approximately 65,000 young people in US juvenile prisons, costing state justice budgets around $5 billion per year. So it isn't surprising that support is growing for a cheaper – and more effective – way to rehabilitate young people who get into trouble or break the law.

A new treatment program called Multisystemic Therapy (MST) can help troubled kids get back on track, without removing them from their homes. It has even helped rehabilitate youth offenders who have served time for committing serious crimes. Heather Robbins, from the American Center for Crime Prevention, said: "Bad behavior may start at home because of family problems, although kids can also get involved with crime if they fall in with the wrong crowd. Locking up teenagers doesn't solve these issues. It's better to deal with the problem at the source."

Ms. Robbins described how MST treated not just the young person, but their whole family, too. "MST therapists advise young people and their parents how to avoid arguments and encourage trust and respect. They also supervise participants at school and in recreational areas," she added. "The therapist arranges activities for them and tells them to stay away from people who are bad influences."

Ms. Robbins explained that MST therapists were available 24 hours a day, and visited participants several times a week for five months. "The treatment can cost around $4,700 for each participant," she said. "But if the young person goes to prison instead, they will be more likely to reoffend in the future. And every young person who is incarcerated will cost society as a whole around $132,000."

However, some people say that MST is too lenient, and that everyone who commits a serious crime should be put behind bars, even if they are under 18. Whether it is right or wrong, MST is proving to be a successful solution to youth crime.

Katie Smith, a 16-year-old from New Jersey, agrees that MST works. She described how she had been convicted of assault the previous year. "The juvenile court ordered me to go to juvenile prison," she said. She admitted that she deserved to be punished, but it was clear that prison didn't help her very much.

In spite of serving five months in prison, when Katie got out, her life hadn't changed. "Mom and I were arguing all the time. I was still in a gang, and I was always skipping school or getting into fights," she recalled. She was assigned an MST therapist, and, three months later, things have improved dramatically.

"I'm going to stay in school, and my mom and I have a better relationship now," she said. "I've apologized for causing problems, and she's promised to be more understanding. I've started playing basketball, and I'm trying to cut myself off from the gang. Our town is small, so I sometimes bump into them, but I think I'll be OK."

Focus on false friends

4. Find these words in the text. Circle the correct definitions.
   1. advise (line 28)
      recommend or suggest / warn or tell
   2. arguments (line 29)
      points or themes of a conversation / conversations where people disagree, often angrily
   3. assigned (line 60)
      given / signed

False friends list pages 60–61

Bad Behavior

Stage 2 Read and understand

5 🔊 1.10 Read the article again. Choose the correct answers.

1 In the US, …
  A incarcerating young people always prevents them from reoffending.
  B 65,000 young people are incarcerated each year.
  C it isn't surprising that young people break the law.
  D there are more young people in prison than in most other countries.
  E $65,000 is spent a year on juvenile prisons.

2 Multisystemic Therapy …
  A treats youth offenders in prison.
  B doesn't take youth offenders from their homes.
  C helps children whose parents are criminals.
  D can't help youth offenders who have committed serious crimes.
  E helps kids who are scared of being in crowds.

3 MST therapists …
  A find it difficult to avoid arguments with participants.
  B don't visit participants very often.
  C visit participants in different places.
  D earn $4,700 per participant.
  E are paid $132,000 by society as a whole.

4 Katie Smith …
  A feels she has benefited from MST.
  B was assaulted last year.
  C should have spent longer in prison.
  D assaulted another teenager in prison.
  E was lucky not to go to prison.

5 Katie …
  A and her mother still argue constantly.
  B has decided to leave school.
  C thinks her mother shouldn't cause problems.
  D plays sports with other members of her gang.
  E doesn't want to be in a gang anymore.

Reading strategy

Using the context

If you don't understand a word, guess its meaning from the context.
1 Read the sentence. Is the word a verb, a noun, an adjective, or an adverb?
2 Think of another word to replace it, without changing the meaning of the sentence.
3 If the word has more than one meaning, use the context to decide which is correct.

6 Read the *Reading strategy* above. Find words 1–4 in the article. What do they mean in this context? Circle A or B.

1 juvenile (line 4)
  A childish, silly
  B relating to young people

2 crowd (line 23)
  A a particular group of people
  B a large number of people in a public place

3 clear (line 54)
  A easy to understand
  B free of unwanted objects

4 gang (line 58)
  A a group of friends who meet regularly
  B a group of people who cause trouble together

Vocabulary

Verbs: crime and criminals

1 Read the quotations. Which are in favor of juvenile prison?

A Juveniles who are **convicted** of serious crimes should be **incarcerated**. They don't deserve to be **rehabilitated** at home. They should be **punished**!

B After being **supervised** at home for four months, Carl has stopped **offending**, and his relationship with his family has improved. This treatment was more effective than putting him behind bars.

C Once the teenager was **arrested**, he was **sentenced** to one year in juvenile prison but **served** only half the time before he was allowed home. The juvenile court was too lenient!

2 Match the **bold** verbs in exercise 1 with definitions 1–9 below.
1 helped to live a normal life after being sick or in prison   _____
2 taken to a police station suspected of a crime   _____
3 given a particular punishment in court   _____
4 watched to make sure they behave properly   _____
5 made to suffer because they have done something wrong   _____
6 spent a period of time (in prison)   _____
7 officially decided in court that someone is guilty of a crime   _____
8 committing crimes   _____
9 put in prison   _____

3 Write the noun forms of the verbs below. Use a dictionary to help you.

1 serve _____   4 rehabilitate _____   7 convict _____
2 sentence _____   5 punish _____   8 offend _____
3 supervise _____   6 incarcerate _____   9 arrest _____

Focus on phrasal verbs

4 Write the infinitive form of the red phrasal verbs in these sentences. Match them with the definitions below.

> become involved with (people) • put in prison •
> meet someone without planning to •
> stop contacting (people)

1 They've **cut** themselves **off** from their families.
2 I think young offenders should be **locked up** for a period of time.
3 We **bumped into** George the other day for the first time in years.
4 Theo has **fallen in with** a group of boys from a different school.

Word list
arrest
convict
incarcerate
offend
punish
rehabilitate
sentence
serve
supervise

bump into
cut (yourself) off
fall in with
lock up

Bad Behavior 8

Language workshop

Reporting verbs

- In reported speech, we use different verbs to report what someone has said.

1 verb + (that)	She **explained that** MST could rehabilitate youth offenders.	added, admitted, agreed, announced, explained, recalled, replied, said
2 verb + object + *to* + infinitive	The court **ordered him to go** to juvenile prison.	advised, asked, invited, ordered, told
3 verb + *to* + infinitive	She's **promised to be** more understanding.	agreed, offered, promised
4 verb + *for* + gerund	I've **apologized for causing** problems.	apologized

Language reference page 79

5 Complete the sentences with the correct reporting verbs.
1. The police officer **said** / **told** that two women had been convicted.
2. Amir **admitted** / **apologized** for behaving so badly.
3. The teacher **announced** / **told** me to wait outside the classroom.
4. The lady **advised** / **recalled** that she had seen the boy outside the store.
5. The girls **agreed** / **invited** to go shopping after school.
6. The therapist **advised** / **said** Ben to listen to his parents.

Expressions of time and place

- In reported speech, we change the expressions of time and place.
  - Direct speech: "I had a meeting **yesterday**," said Eva.
  - Reported speech: Eva said that she had had a meeting **the day before**.

  - Direct speech: "We'll visit **this** family **tomorrow**," they agreed.
  - Reported speech: They agreed to visit **that** family **the next day**.

Language reference page 79

6 Complete the chart with the expressions of time and place below.

this / these • the next day • last night • ~~that day~~ • the day before • here • then • the following week

Direct speech	Reported speech
today	*that day*
yesterday	1 _____
tomorrow	2 _____
3 _____	the previous night

Direct speech	Reported speech
next week	4 _____
now	5 _____
6 _____	there
7 _____	that / those

Vocabulary Get it right

Correct the errors in these sentences.

This unit
1. Amy has been served to two months in prison.
2. Leo admitted for he had been skipping school.
3. The police officers agreed to release the boy next day.

Previous unit
4. Last week we installed an apple tree in our yard.
5. You can borrow or the red shoes or the blue ones.
6. Without proper insulate houses can be very cold.

Grammar

Stage 1 Get ready!

1 Read the chart. Look back at the text on page 50. Find more examples of reported speech. Which categories do they belong to?

Reported speech

When we change between direct speech and reported speech, we …
- change the tense of the main verb (see the *Language extra* below).
- change the pronouns and expressions of time and place.
- remove the quotation marks.

	Direct speech	Reported speech
Statements	"Kids **fall** in with the wrong crowd," said Heather.	→ Heather said (that) kids **fell** in with the wrong crowd.
	"The court **offered** me MST," said Katie.	→ Katie said (that) the court **had offered** her MST.
	"I**'ve apologized** for causing problems," she said.	→ She said (that) she **had apologized** for causing problems.
	"I**'m going** to stay in school," she said.	→ She said (that) she **was going** to stay in school.
	"I**'ll** be OK," she said.	→ She said (that) she **would** be OK.
Questions	"Why **did** you **argue** with your mom?" the therapist asked Katie.	→ The therapist asked Katie why she **had argued** with her mom.
	"What **is** your favorite sport?" the therapist asked Katie.	→ The therapist asked Katie what her favorite sport **was**.
	"**Do** you **want** to join the basketball team?" the coach asked her.	→ The coach asked her **if / whether** she **wanted** to join the basketball team.
Orders	"**Stay** away from these people!"	→ The therapist told the child **to stay away** from those people.
	"**Don't be** so rude!"	→ Katie's mom told her **not to be** so rude.
Suggestions	"Why don't you **try** a new sport?" he suggested to Katie.	→ He suggested **that she try** a new sport. (**tries** ✗)
	"Let's **have** a talk with Katie," she suggested.	→ She suggested **having** a talk with Katie.

Language reference page 78

Stage 2 Practice

2 Read the *Language extra*. Write the reported statements as direct statements.

The man told the boys that someone had written graffiti on his wall.
"Someone has written graffiti on my wall," the man told the boys.

1 The boys replied that they hadn't done it.
"We _____"

2 They added that they had only just arrived.
"We _____"

3 The man said that he thought they were lying.
"I _____"

4 The boys said that he couldn't prove it.
"You _____"

5 The man said that he would have to call the police.
"I _____"

Language extra

- We change the verb tenses between direct speech and reported speech like this:

Direct speech	→	Reported speech
simple present	→	simple past
present continuous	→	past continuous
present perfect	→	past perfect
simple past	→	past perfect
past perfect	→	past perfect
will	→	would
can	→	could

Bad Behavior 8

3 Rewrite the direct statements as reported statements.

"I began offending as a teenager," the man said.
The man said _he had begun offending as a teenager._

1 "No one's listening to me!" she complained.
   She complained _____
2 "I've arranged a meeting with a new client," Estela said.
   Estela said _____
3 "I hate being in prison," Gaspar said.
   Gaspar _____
4 "You can stay with your family," the judge told Luis.
   The judge _____
5 "Our daughter was out of control," they explained.
   They _____

4 Put the words in order to make reported questions.

asked / The girls / Lisa / she wanted / with them / if / to hang out
The girls asked Lisa if she wanted to hang out with them.

1 he / OK / Ben / asked / I / would be / if
   _____
2 where / The therapist / I had lived / asked / before / me
   _____
3 She / our grandmother / how / was / asked / us
   _____
4 my favorite subject / The teacher / was / me / what / asked
   _____
5 He / whether / he could / asked / Silvia / call her
   _____

5 Rewrite the orders as reported orders.

"Don't be late." Mom told me _not to be late._

1 "Walk slowly." The teacher told the children _____
2 "Don't be noisy." The teacher told them _____
3 "Leave the room." She told us _____
4 "Don't worry about me." Emma told Sara _____
5 "Stop hanging out with those people," I told Luke _____

6 Write the correct form of the verb in parentheses.

1 I suggest that you _____ carefully. (**listen**)
2 Carla suggested _____ the party. (**cancel**)
3 Mom suggested that I _____ to bed early. (**go**)
4 We suggested _____ a teacher. (**tell**)
5 Michael suggested _____ something to eat. (**get**)
6 The teacher suggested that we _____ hard for the test. (**study**)

Grammar   Get it right

Correct the errors in these sentences.

This unit
1 She said she will go tomorrow.
2 Dad told you don't to leave your bag on the floor.
3 I asked her where did she live.

Previous unit
4 I think the parents should be tell.
5 Jessica will visited by a trained therapist.
6 The man has been arrested from the police.

Language Reference

Essentials

Tenses

Tense or structure	Affirmative	Negative	Interrogative	Use
Simple present	I/You/We/They **work**. He/She/It **works**.	I/You/We/They **do not work**. He/She/It **does not work**.	**Do** I/you/we/they **work**? **Does** he/she/it **work**?	• facts, permanent situations • habits, repeated actions • stative verbs
Present continuous	I **am working**. He/She/It **is working**. You/We/They **are working**.	I **am not working**. He/She/It **is not working**. You/We/They **are not working**.	**Am** I **working**? **Is** he/she/it **working**? **Are** you/we/they **working**?	• actions happening now • temporary situations • future use, to talk about plans and personal arrangements
Present perfect simple	I/You/We/They **have worked**. He/She/It **has worked**.	I/You/We/They **have not worked**. He/She/It **has not worked**.	**Have** I/you/we/they **worked**? **Has** he/she/it **worked**?	• present situations that started in the past • past experiences, without saying exactly when they happened
Present perfect continuous	I/You/We/They **have been working**. He/She/It **has been working**.	I/You/We/They **have not been working**. He/She/It **has not been working**.	**Have** I/you/we/they **been working**? **Has** he/she/it **been working**?	• present situations that started in the past • past actions or situations with an effect on the present
Simple past	I/You/He/She/It/We/They **worked**.	I/You/He/She/It/We/They **did not work**.	**Did** I/you/he/she/it/we/they **work**?	• completed actions or events in the past • things which happened repeatedly in the past • past states
Past continuous	I/He/She/It **was working**. You/We/They **were working**.	I/He/She/It **was not working**. You/We/They **were not working**.	**Was** I/he/she/it **working**? **Were** you/we/they **working**?	• actions in progress at a specific time in the past • past actions interrupted by other actions
Past perfect	I/You/He/She/It/We/They **had worked**.	I/You/He/She/It/We/They **had not worked**.	**Had** I/you/he/she/it/we/they **worked**?	• states or actions that happened before other events in the past
used to	I/You/He/She/It/We/They **used to work**.	I/You/He/She/It/We/They **did not use to work**.	**Did** I/you/he/she/it/we/they **use to work**?	• past habits or situations that are no longer true in the present
will for future use	I/You/He/She/It/We/They **will work**.	I/You/He/She/It/We/They **won't** (= will not) **work**.	**Will** I/you/he/she/it/we/they **work**?	• making predictions or giving opinions about the future • spontaneous decisions
be going to for future use	I **am going to work**. He/She/It **is going to work**. You/We/They **are going to work**.	I **am not going to work**. He/She/It **is not going to work**. You/We/They **are not going to work**.	**Am** I **going to work**? **Is** he/she/it **going to work**? **Are** you/we/they **going to work**?	• predictions based on evidence • plans and intentions

Language Reference

Time expressions

Time expressions	Use
an hour / day / week / month ago last week / month / year / Tuesday yesterday morning / evening	• with the **simple past** — *He left last week.*
when while	• to link **simple past** and **past continuous** clauses — *He left while it was raining.* — *When he left, it was raining.*
for, since already, just, yet, still never, ever	• with the **present perfect** — *He has been here since midnight.*
after, before until as soon as	• to link **simple past** clauses — *He put on his shoes before he went out.*

Modals

Modal verb / structure	Use
can / can't could / couldn't be able to / not be able to	• to talk about ability
must	• to express certainty
may / may not (NOT mayn't) could might / mightn't	• to express possibility
can't	• to express impossibility
have to / must	• to express obligation
don't have to (NOT must not)	• to say something is not obligatory
must not	• to express prohibition
should / shouldn't ought to	• to give advice • to make recommendations

Modal perfect	Use
must have + past participle	• to express a certainty in the past
can't have + past participle	• to express an impossibility in the past
may / might have + past participle	• to express a possibility in the past
could have + past participle	• to suggest an alternative past action
should have + past participle	• to express a criticism of a past action

Verbs + prepositions

Form	Examples
verb + *at*	arrive, guess, laugh, look
verb + *in*	arrive, believe, result, succeed
verb + *of*	accuse, approve, dream, take care, think
verb + *on*	concentrate, depend, insist, rely, spend
verb + *to*	belong, get married, happen, listen
verb + *for*	apologize, apply, care, look, pay, wait
verb + *from*	benefit, differ, resign, result, suffer
verb + *with*	agree, argue, meet, speak, talk, visit
verb + *about*	agree, argue, care, complain, dream, talk, think, worry

Gerunds and infinitives

Verbs	Followed by …
admit, avoid, can't stand, can't imagine, consider, don't mind, enjoy, finish, imagine, mention, miss, practice, report, suggest	gerund
afford, agree, arrange, ask, choose, decide, expect, hope, learn, manage, pretend, promise, seem, tempt, want	*to* + infinitive
begin, hate, like, love, prefer, start	gerund OR *to* + infinitive (same meaning)
regret, stop, remember, forget	gerund OR *to* + infinitive (different meaning)

Conditionals

Form	Use
Zero conditional <*if* + simple present>, <simple present> OR <simple present> <*if* + simple present>	• things that are always true, for example, scientific facts — *If you boil water, it turns to steam.*
First conditional <*if* + simple present>, <*will* + infinitive> OR <*will* + infinitive> <*if* + simple present>	• possible or probable future events — *If you do that again, I'll be angry.*
Second conditional <*if* + simple past>, <*would* + infinitive> OR <*would* + infinitive> <*if* + simple past>	• hypothetical present or future events — *If I knew where he lived, I would visit him.*
Third conditional <*if* + past perfect>, <*would have* + past participle> OR <*would have* + past participle> <*if* + past perfect>	• hypothetical events in the past — *If I'd worked harder, I would have passed my exam.*

Relative clauses

Relative pronoun	Use
when	• to refer to times
where	• to refer to places
which / that	• to refer to things
who / that	• to refer to people
whose	• to express possession

Relative clause	Form	Use
Defining relative clause	She's the girl **who helped me**.	• to give essential information about the noun that they follow
Non-defining relative clause	The girl**, who was very clever,** helped me.	• to give extra, non-essential information about the noun that they follow

The passive

Tense	Active	Passive
Simple present	open	is opened
Present continuous	is opening	is being opened
Present perfect	has opened	has been opened
Simple past	opened	was opened
Past continuous	was opening	was being opened
Past perfect	had opened	had been opened
will	will open	will be opened
be going to	is going to open	is going to be opened
Modals	may / must / can open	may / must / can be opened

We use the passive to emphasize the action (= the verb) more than the person who did the action (= the agent).

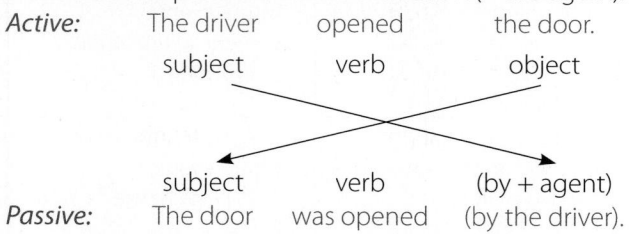

Active: The driver opened the door.
        subject   verb   object

Passive: The door was opened (by the driver).
        subject   verb   (by + agent)

Reported speech: tense changes

Direct speech	→	Reported speech
Simple present He said, "I eat."	→	**Simple past** He said he ate.
Present continuous He said, "I'm eating."	→	**Past continuous** He said he was eating.
Present perfect He said, "I have eaten."	→	**Past perfect** He said he had eaten.
Simple past He said, "I ate."	→	**Past perfect** He said he had eaten.
will He said, "I'll eat."	→	*would* He said he would eat.
can He said, "I can eat."	→	*could* He said he could eat.
must He said, "I must eat."	→	*have to* He said he had to eat.

Reported speech: time expression changes

Direct speech	→	Reported speech
now	→	then
today	→	that day
tonight	→	that night
tomorrow	→	the next OR following day
next week / month / year	→	the next OR following week / month / year
yesterday	→	the day before
last night / week / month / year	→	the night / week / month / year before OR the previous night / week / month / year

Reported speech: reporting verbs

Structure	Example
verb + (*that*) add, admit, agree, announce, declare, explain, insist, recall, recommend, reply, report, reveal, say, suggest	He **admitted (that)** he was wrong.
verb + object + *to* + infinitive advise, ask, invite, order, remind, tell	She **asked me to help**.
verb + *to* + infinitive agree, decide, offer, promise, refuse, threaten	She **decided to leave**.

Irregular verbs

Language Reference

Infinitive	Simple past	Past participle	Infinitive	Simple past	Past participle
be	was / were	been	lie (= posture)	lay	lain
beat	beat	beaten	lie (= untruth)	lied	lied
become	became	become	light	lit, lighted	lit, lighted
begin	began	begun	lose	lost	lost
bend	bent	bent	make	made	made
bet	bet	bet	mean	meant	meant
bite	bit	bitten	meet	met	met
bleed	bled	bled	pay	paid	paid
blow	blew	blown	put	put	put
break	broke	broken	read	read	read
bring	brought	brought	ride	rode	ridden
broadcast	broadcast	broadcast	ring	rang	rung
build	built	built	rise	rose	risen
burn	burned, burnt	burned, burnt	run	ran	run
buy	bought	bought	say	said	said
catch	caught	caught	see	saw	seen
choose	chose	chosen	sell	sold	sold
come	came	come	send	sent	sent
cost	cost	cost	shake	shook	shaken
cut	cut	cut	shine	shone	shone
dig	dug	dug	shoot	shot	shot
do	did	done	show	showed	shown
draw	drew	drawn	shut	shut	shut
dream	dreamed, dreamt	dreamed, dreamt	sing	sang	sung
drink	drank	drunk	sink	sank	sunk
drive	drove	driven	sit	sat	sat
eat	ate	eaten	sleep	slept	slept
fall	fell	fallen	smell	smelled, smelt	smelled, smelt
feed	fed	fed	speak	spoke	spoken
feel	felt	felt	spell	spelled, spelt	spelled, spelt
fight	fought	fought	spend	spent	spent
find	found	found	spin	spun, span	spun
flee	fled	fled	spill	spilled, spilt	spilled, spilt
fly	flew	flown	split	split	split
forbid	forbade	forbidden	spoil	spoiled, spoilt	spoiled, spoilt
forget	forgot	forgotten	spread	spread	spread
forgive	forgave	forgiven	spring	sprang	sprung
freeze	froze	frozen	stand	stood	stood
get	got	gotten, got	steal	stole	stolen
give	gave	given	stick	stuck	stuck
go	went	gone / been*	sting	stung	stung
grow	grew	grown	strike	struck	struck
hang	hung	hung	sweep	swept	swept
have	had	had	swim	swam	swum
hear	heard	heard	swing	swung	swung
hit	hit	hit	take	took	taken
hold	held	held	teach	taught	taught
hurt	hurt	hurt	tear	tore	torn
keep	kept	kept	tell	told	told
know	knew	known	think	thought	thought
lay	laid	laid	throw	threw	thrown
lead	led	led	understand	understood	understood
learn	learned, learnt	learned, learnt	wake	woke	woken
leave	left	left	wear	wore	worn
lend	lent	lent	win	won	won
let	let	let	write	wrote	written

*see page 64

False friends

This list includes some of the most common false friends for speakers of Latin languages. Sometimes, the differences in meaning can be small, but very important. Some words can be cognates or false friends, depending on the context.

False friend	Definition	Example
accent (n)	way of pronouncing words	She speaks Portuguese with a strong American **accent**.
actual (adj)	real; exact	What were his **actual** words?
actually (adv)	really; in fact	What did she **actually** say?
		Actually, I don't agree with you.
adept (adj)	good at something	Politicians have to be **adept** at public speaking.
adequate (adj)	good enough; sufficient	Your work is **adequate**, but you could do better.
admire (v)	respect	I don't agree with her, but I **admire** her principles.
advertise (v)	promote a product for sale	They **advertised** their new CD on TV.
advice (n)	help and suggestions	I didn't know what to do, but Mom gave me some **advice**.
advise (v)	recommend or suggest	She was in pain, so I **advised** her to see a doctor.
advocate (n)	a person who supports a plan or action	**Advocates** of the council's plan say it will improve infrastructure.
amass (v)	collect something in large quantities	Over ten years, they have **amassed** a fortune from their business.
anticipate (v)	expect something and prepare for it	I **anticipate** that the situation will get worse.
anxious (adj)	worried	She was **anxious** about the exam tomorrow.
appoint (v)	give a job or role to someone	The committee has **appointed** a new director.
argument (n)	conversation where people disagree, often angrily	They had a terrible **argument** and he left.
assign (v)	give someone something that they can use, or work on	The teacher **assigned** a task to each group of students.
assist (v)	help	How can I **assist** you, sir?
assume (v)	suppose that something is true	I **assume** that you have the necessary documents.
attend (v)	go to; be present at	I won't be able to **attend** tonight's meeting.
audience (n)	spectators	The **audience** was wild with excitement.
balcony (n)	platform that is built on the outside wall of a building	When the weather is fine, we often eat out on the **balcony**.
brave (adj)	courageous	This might hurt a little, so try to be **brave**.
cast (n)	all the people who act in a play or movie	This movie has an excellent **cast**.
casual (adj)	relaxed; not smart	Don't wear **casual** clothes for a job interview.
casualty (n)	victim of an accident or war	The army retreated after suffering heavy **casualties**.
certain (adj)	completely sure; without any doubts	We are absolutely **certain** that the explosion was an accident.
college (n)	university; place of higher education	He's studying Law at **college**.
commodity (n)	product or material that you can sell	Salt used to be a very valuable **commodity**.
comprehensive (adj)	including everything	This book gives **comprehensive** information on the subject.
compromise (n)	agreement where both sides have to give something up	After hours of argument, the two sides finally reached a **compromise**.
confidence (n)	certainty about your abilities and qualities	The public is losing **confidence** in the government.
conform (v)	follow customs; be the same as others	She was a real individual and did not **conform**.
consequently (adv)	as a result	She didn't study hard and **consequently** failed the test.
content (adj)	satisfied with what you have	He is **content** with a small house and a modest salary.
control (v)	have power over someone or something	Some parents find it difficult to **control** their children.
convenient (adj)	easy or quick to do	These meals are quick and **convenient** to prepare.
costume (n)	traditional or historical clothes; clothes worn by an actor or at a party	He went to the party in a giant chicken **costume**.
crave (v)	have a strong desire for something	She's an anxious child who **craves** attention.
current (adj)	present; happening now	We're worried about the **current** economic situation.
data (n)	facts or information used to find out things or to make decisions	The research team has collected **data** from 40 countries.
deception (n)	making someone believe a lie	He was accused of obtaining property by **deception**.
discuss (v)	talk about a subject; debate	We **discussed** possible ideas for our group project.
disgusted (adj)	shocked; strongly disapproving	I was **disgusted** at the way they treated those animals.
diversion (n)	change of direction; alternative route	We made a short **diversion** to go and look at the castle.
education (n)	schooling	Students get an excellent **education** at this college.
effectively (adv)	with good results	It was a difficult situation, but you handled it very **effectively**.
eventually (adv)	finally; in the end	The flight was five hours late, but **eventually** we arrived.
exit (n)	way out	Excuse me, where's the museum **exit**?
expert (n)	person with special knowledge, skills, or training	He is an **expert** in child psychology.
exquisite (adj)	extremely beautiful or finely made	She was wearing an **exquisite** silver necklace.
fabric (n)	material used for making clothes, etc.	The curtains were made of plain cotton **fabric**.
form (v)	create; give shape to	We **formed** a rock band at school.

Language Reference

False friend	Definition	Example
genial (adj)	friendly and cheerful	He greeted us at the door with a **genial** smile.
grip (n)	strong hold	You won't fall if you keep a tight **grip** on the rope.
groceries (n)	food and other goods sold in a supermarket	This store will deliver your **groceries** to your home.
humor (n)	ability to laugh at things	You need a great sense of **humor** to be a professional comedian.
idiom (n)	linguistic expression with a special meaning	"Be in luck" is an **idiom** that means "be fortunate".
ingenuity (n)	quality of being clever, original, and inventive	His new invention displays great **ingenuity**.
injury (n)	harm or damage done to your body	They escaped from the accident with only minor **injuries**.
instance (n)	particular case or example of something	Normally I agree with you, but in this **instance** I think you're wrong.
introduce (v)	give the name of a new person or thing	Let me **introduce** you to my friends.
journal (n)	specialist magazine	Her article was published in a prestigious medical **journal**.
journey (n)	long trip	In May they set off on their **journey** across Asia.
large (adj)	big	I'll have a cheeseburger and a **large** soda, please.
lecture (n)	talk given by an expert; class at college	He gave a **lecture** on the geology of the Pacific.
legend (n)	very famous person	She's become a **legend** in the world of jazz music.
library (n)	place where you borrow books	I returned my books to the **library**.
location (n)	place where a movie or TV show is filmed	They're filming at a secret **location** in Mexico.
magazine (n)	regular publication containing articles, photos, etc.	I like reading fashion **magazines**.
major (adj)	very large or important	There haven't been any **major** problems.
miserable (adj)	very sad	You look **miserable**. What's wrong?
misery (n)	extreme sadness; suffering	There was an expression of pain and **misery** on his face.
nervous (adj)	afraid or fearful	I always get **nervous** just before an exam.
notes (n)	written words that help you remember	The teacher told us to take **notes** in class.
notice (n)	written or printed announcement	There's a **notice** on the wall giving the opening times.
ordinary (adj)	common; not unusual	They are just **ordinary** people like you and me.
parents (n)	mother and father	He's still living with his **parents**.
particular (adj)	specific	On that **particular** day I wasn't at school.
prejudice (n)	unreasonable preference or dislike	He has a **prejudice** against female doctors.
present (v)	give something to someone	The principal **presented** a trophy to the winning team.
pretend (v)	act falsely; give a false appearance	She **pretended** to be 18, but she was only 16.
prevent (v)	stop something from happening	Wearing sunblock **prevents** getting sunburn.
professor (n)	specialist teacher at a university	He became a Harvard **professor** at the age of 40.
prove (v)	show that something is true	It will be difficult to **prove** that she is innocent.
push (v)	use your hands or body to move something away from you	We **pushed** the table into the corner of the room.
quiet (adj)	making very little noise	You have to be **quiet** when you're working in the library.
rare (adj)	not very common	This species of bird is very **rare**. It was last seen 20 years ago.
realize (v)	perceive; become aware of	When I got home, I **realized** I had lost my cell phone.
recipient (n)	person who receives something	The **recipients** of this year's prize are Jorge and Maribel.
record (v)	copy or keep an account of something	I forgot to **record** my favorite TV show last night!
requirement (n)	something that you need, or must do	What is the minimum entrance **requirement** for this college?
rest (v)	relax after an activity	The doctor told me I have to **rest** for three months!
resume (v)	start something again	We **resumed** our conversation after a brief interruption.
retail (n)	the selling of goods to the public, usually through stores	The recommended **retail** price of this dishwasher is $530.
retire (v)	stop doing your job (usually because of old age)	She **retired** early, at the age of 50.
rude (adj)	disrespectful; impolite; offensive	It's **rude** to interrupt when other people are speaking.
sane (adj)	not crazy	I'm not mad! I'm completely **sane**!
sensible (adj)	not silly; with good judgment	He's very **sensible**; you can trust him to behave.
stranger (n)	person that you don't know	I had to ask a **stranger** to help me with my luggage.
suburb (n)	residential area that is not in the center of a city	They lived in a big house in a smart, modern **suburb**.
support (v)	help or encourage	My friends have **supported** me through some difficult times.
sympathetic (adj)	kind and understanding; good at listening	He was very **sympathetic** about my problem.
terrific (adj)	extremely good	You're doing a **terrific** job! Well done!
topic (n)	subject that people talk about	I tried hard to think of another **topic** of conversation.
translate (v)	change words into another language	This book has been **translated** into Quechua.
ultimate (adj)	most impressive	For me, the **ultimate** luxury is to stay in bed all day.
ultimately (adv)	in the end; at the most basic level	A poor diet will **ultimately** lead to health problems.
vegetable (n)	plant eaten as food	We need to eat plenty of **vegetables** for a healthy diet.
vicious (adj)	violent and cruel	The victims suffered a **vicious** and brutal attack.
vulgar (adj)	impolite; offensive	They were offended by his **vulgar** jokes.

Starter unit

Simple present

Structure

See *Essentials* page 56.

Use

We use the simple present to talk about:
- facts and permanent situations.
  He **lives** in Rio.
  She **speaks** French.
- habits and repeated actions.
  I **play soccer** every weekend.
  She usually **meets** friends after work.
- mental and emotional states, including senses, opinions, and feelings.
  I **feel** sad.
  Helen **thinks** it's a good idea.
  We **like** traveling.

> We use stative verbs, including *like, love, prefer, enjoy, hate, can't stand* to talk about mental and emotional states. Stative verbs do not normally use the continuous form.
> He **likes** rock music
> NOT He**'s liking** rock music.

Present continuous

Structure

See *Essentials* page 56.

Use

We use the present continuous to talk about:
- actions in progress now.
  I**'m waiting** for Tim.
  Right now, she**'s watching** TV.
- temporary situations.
  My brother**'s working** in Mexico right now.
  She**'s studying** for her exams at the moment.

> We cannot use the simple present to talk about actions in progress now.
> "What **are** you **doing**?" "I**'m calling** my mom!"
> NOT "What **do** you **do**?" "I **call** my mom!"
> What**'s happening**?
> NOT What **happens**?
> Excuse me, I**'m looking** for the bus stop.
> NOT Excuse me, I look for the bus stop.

> With some verbs we do not normally use the continuous form. These are called stative verbs. The most common are:
> - verbs that express state or possession: *be, have, own*
>   She **isn't** very well.
>   His father **owns** three cars.
> - verbs that express thoughts and opinions: *believe, know, understand, remember, forget, think*
>   I **remember** his name.
>   They **know** where you live.
> - verbs that express likes or preferences: *like, love, prefer, enjoy, hate, can't stand.* We normally use these with nouns or with gerunds.
>   I **hate** horror movies.
>   He **loves** jazz music.
>   She **enjoys** reading.

Simple past

Structure

See *Essentials* page 56.

Use

We use the simple past to talk about:
- completed actions or events in the past. This is useful in narratives, to describe a sequence of events.
  Sam **opened** the door.
  What time **did** you **arrive**?
  When I **got** to the theater, I **bought** a ticket.
- past states.
  She **was** very unhappy.
  They **didn't believe** me.
- things which happened repeatedly in the past.
  We **called** Grandma every Sunday night.
  I **went** to the mall three times last week.

Past continuous

Structure

See *Essentials* page 56.

Use

We use the past continuous to talk about:
- actions in progress at a specific time in the past.
  At two o'clock, I **was driving** home.
  Yesterday morning we **were taking** a test.
- past actions which are interrupted by another action.
  He **was talking to** his girlfriend when I arrived.
  I **was waiting** at the bus stop when he saw me.

Language Reference

Simple past and past continuous

Contrast

We use the simple past to talk about a finished action in the past.

We use the past continuous to talk about an action in progress, but not finished, at a specific time in the past.
I **made** dinner last night. I **started** at eight fifteen and I **finished** at ten to nine.
(finished actions = simple past)
"What **were** you **doing** at eight thirty?" "I **was making** dinner."
(actions in progress at a specific time = past continuous)

We can combine the simple past and the past continuous with **when** and **while**. We can change the order of the two tenses.
While I **was eating**, the phone **rang**.
= The phone **rang while** I **was eating**.
When the phone **rang**, I **was eating**.
= I **was eating when** the phone **rang**.

used to

Structure

See *Essentials* page 56.

Use

We use **used to** to talk about past actions, habits, or situations that are no longer true in the present.
She **used to like** him. (but she doesn't any more)
We **used to go** to the same school. (but now we don't)

> We can use the simple past OR **used to** to describe repeated actions, habits, or situations in the past. Both refer to an indefinite time in the past, but **used to** tells us that that the action, habit, or situation doesn't happen now.
> I **used to** enjoy playing tennis when I was younger. (I don't enjoy it any more)
> I **enjoyed** playing tennis when I was younger. (maybe I still enjoy it, maybe not)
>
> If we are talking about one finished action, or one finished period, at a specific time in the past, we have to use the simple past, NOT **used to**.
> I **lived** in Recife **for** four years.
> NOT ~~I used to live in Recife for four years.~~
> We **went** to a baseball game last week.
> NOT ~~We used to go to a baseball game last week.~~

do and *make*

In order to write and speak natural, accurate English, you need to learn collocations: for example, which nouns commonly go with which verbs.

Many nouns collocate with the verbs *do* and *make*. There are no rules, so you will need to use a dictionary and learn them. You will find a list of some of the most common collocations with *do* and *make* in the Wordlist on page 80.

Phrasal verbs

Phrasal verbs are verbs made of two or three words. The first word is the main verb. After the main verb is an adverb (**split up**), or a preposition (**deal with**), or both (**get on with**). These adverbs or prepositions are sometimes called particles.

The meaning of a phrasal verb is often different from the meanings of the separate parts.

Phrasal verbs are very common in English, especially in spoken and informal English.

To find the meaning of phrasal verbs, use a dictionary. Phrasal verbs are usually listed with the main verb. For example, to find the meaning of **let down**, you should look for **let** in your dictionary.

Here are some common phrasal verbs that we use to talk about relationships:
ask (someone) out
break up with (someone)
fall for (someone)
get on with (someone)
get over (someone, something)
go out with (someone)
let (someone) down

Some phrasal verbs are separable. This means we can put the object between the two parts of the phrasal verb.

- When the object is a pronoun or a person's name, we put it between the two parts of the phrasal verb.
  She doesn't want to **let** him **down**.
  She doesn't want to **let** Peter **down**.
  NOT ~~She doesn't want to let down him.~~
  AND NOT USUALLY ~~She doesn't want to let down Peter.~~

- When the object is a noun, we can put it between the two parts of the phrasal verb or after the particle.
  She doesn't want to **let** the team **down**.
  OR She doesn't want to **let down** the team.

Unit 1

Present perfect simple

Structure

Affirmative		
I/you/we/they	+ have (= 've)	+ past participle
he/she/it	+ has (= 's)	

She**'s lived** in New York for four years.
We **have** never **been** to Florida.

Negative		
I/you/we/they	+ have not (= haven't)	+ past participle
he/she/it	+ has not (= hasn't)	

I **haven't been** to Chile.
He **hasn't sold** his house.

Interrogative		
Have	+ I/you/we/they	+ past participle ?
Has	+ he/she/it	

Have you **been** to Europe?
Has she **moved** into her new apartment?

> Regular past participles have the same form as the simple past (see page 56). Learn the irregular verbs on page 59.

> We often use *been* (instead of *gone*) as the past participle of *go*, when we are talking about completed events.
> Laura has **been** to Spain. (she went and came back)
> Laura has **gone** to Spain. (she's still there)

Use

We use the present perfect simple to talk about:

- actions or situations in the past which change the present, or have an effect on the present.
  Someone **has broken** the heater! (it's broken now; it wasn't broken before)
  They**'ve lost** their keys, and they can't get into the house! (they don't have their keys now)
- actions or situations that started in the past and are still continuing now.
  How long **have** you **had** solar panels?
  He **hasn't seen** his sister for four years.
- past experiences, when we do not use a time reference.
  We**'ve lived** in a lot of different places.
  I**'ve** never **met** a movie star.

Present perfect continuous

Structure

Affirmative		
I/you/we/they	+ have (= 've)	+ been + -ing
he/she/it	+ has (= 's)	

He **has been living** in the US for two years.
You **have been playing** computer games all morning.

Negative		
I/you/we/they	+ have not (= haven't)	+ been + -ing
he/she/it	+ has not (= hasn't)	

I **haven't been working** today.
She **hasn't been listening** to you.

Interrogative		
Have	+ I/you/we/they	+ been + -ing
Has	+ he/she/it	

Have you **been using** my computer?
Has she **been living** here for long?

Use

We use the present perfect continuous:

- to talk about a very recent action that affects the present, especially if it is a prolonged or repeated action.
  They're tired because they**'ve been looking** at houses all weekend.
  My hair's wet because it**'s been raining**.
- to emphasize the duration of an action that started in the past and continues in the present.
  I**'ve been cleaning** the house all morning!
- with the time expressions *for* and *since*, to say how long an action or situation has been continuing up to now.
  I**'ve been working** in the city for 20 years.

> We never use present tenses to talk about the duration of an action.
> Henry **has been living** here since 1998.
> NOT Henry is living here since 1998.
> AND NOT Henry lives here since 1998.

> We can use *for* and *since* with the present perfect continuous, especially in reply to the question "How long …?"
> "**How long have** you **been working** here?" "I**'ve been working** here for a month."
> "**How long has** he **been living** abroad?" "He**'s been living** abroad since 2010."

Language Reference 1

Present perfect simple and continuous

Contrast

We use the present perfect simple to emphasize **finished experiences** in our life up to now. We can mention the number of times we have had the experience, but we do not say exactly when.
I've stayed in this hotel twice. (twice in my life up to now; it isn't important exactly when)

We use the present perfect continuous to emphasize the **duration** of an action. At the time of speaking, the action is not complete.
I've been staying at this hotel for two weeks. (two weeks up to now, and I'm still here)
I've been staying at this hotel since February. (several months up to now, and I'm still here)

We use the present perfect simple to emphasize the **finished result** of an action.
I've painted my room. (it's finished now)

We use the present perfect continuous to emphasize the **action**, not the result. We are saying how we have occupied our time. The action can be finished or unfinished.
I've been painting my room all afternoon! (I haven't had time to do other things)

> We don't use the present perfect continuous with stative verbs. The most important stative verbs are: *be*, *have* (= possess), *hate*, *know*, *like*, *love*, *mean*, *need*, *prefer*, *seem*, *understand* and *want*. With these verbs, we have to use the present perfect simple.
> He**'s been** here since Sunday.
> NOT ~~He's been being here since Sunday.~~
> They**'ve** only **known** each other for a few days.
> NOT ~~They've only been knowing ...~~

> When we talk about very long, unchanging situations in the past up to now, we prefer to use the present perfect simple.
> **I've been standing** in this line for hours! (I'm emphasizing that it's a long time, but I know that it's a temporary situation)
> BUT Christ the Redeemer **has stood** over the city of Rio de Janeiro since 1931. (it's been there for a long time, and it's permanent)
> BETTER THAN Christ the Redeemer **has been standing** over the city of Rio de Janeiro since 1931.

so ... that / such ... that

We can use *so ... that* to describe an exceptional quality of a person or thing, and the consequence.
It was **so heavy that** I couldn't lift it.
The chairs were **so expensive that** we couldn't afford them.

- After the adjective you use a *that* clause.
  I was **so tired that** I couldn't stay awake.
- We can also use *so ... that* with an adverb.
  The room is **so large that** it's difficult to heat.

We can also use *such ... that* with a noun group (*a / an* + adjective + noun) in a similar way to *so ... that*.
He had **such a good time that** he wanted to stay.
It's **such a cramped room that** my closet won't fit.

We do not use *a / an* in front of uncountable nouns or plural nouns.
It was **such strong coffee that** I couldn't drink it.
They were **such good friends that** they met for lunch every day.

Conjunctions of purpose: *so that, in order to, to, so as to*

Use

We use conjunctions of purpose to explain why somebody does something.
- We use *so (that)* before a clause (for example, subject + verb).
  He sold his house **so (that) he could move back in with his parents.**
- We use *to*, *in order to*, and *so as to* before an infinitive.
  He sold his house **to / in order to / so as to** move back in with his parents.

Unit 2

Modal verbs

Use

Modal verbs are verbs with unique characteristics. They work with the main verb to add extra meaning, for example, obligation or permission. Many modal verbs have different meanings, depending on their context.

Structure

Modal verbs share the following characteristics:
- We use an infinitive without *to* after modal verbs.
  I **can** speak Italian.
  She **might** be successful.
  BUT He **ought to** work harder.
- Modal verbs do not take *-s* in the third person.
  He **can** drive a car.
  NOT He cans drive a car.
- Modal verbs do not use the auxiliary verb *do / does* to form negatives, questions, or short answers.
  She **might not** know the answer.
  "**Can** you speak English?" "Yes, I **can**."
  NOT "Do you can speak English?" "Yes, I do."
  "**Should** I trust him?" "Yes, you **should**."
- Modal verbs only have one form. To express different tenses, we sometimes have to use other verbs with similar meanings.
  She **might move** to Brazil.
  → She **is probably going to move** to Brazil.

Ability: *can, could, be able to*

We use the modal verb *can* + infinitive (without *to*) to talk about ability in the present.
I **can play** the piano.
He **can't dance**.

We use the modal verb *could* + infinitive (without *to*) to talk about ability in the simple past.
I **could swim** when I was five years old.
He **couldn't walk** until he was three.

There is no future form of *can* or *could*. We use *be able to* + infinitive to talk about ability in the future.
I'**ll be able to meet** you tomorrow.
NOT I'll can meet you tomorrow.
They **won't be able to join** until May.

We can also use *be able to* to talk about ability in the simple past, present perfect, or past perfect.
I **wasn't able to help**.
They **haven't been able to fix** the problem.
We **hadn't been able to leave** the house.

Possibility and deduction: *could, may, might, must, can't*

We use *may, may not, might, might not,* and *could* to talk about present or future possibility.
It **could** be a great opportunity.

You **might not** get an interview.
NOT It can be a great opportunity.

We use *can't* and *must* to make logical deductions.
- We use *can't* when we believe or guess that something is impossible.
  That **can't** be Gustavo. He's too short.
- We use *must* when we are certain something is true.
  She has a bodyguard: she **must** be famous.

Obligation and prohibition: *must, have to*

We use *must* and *have to* to talk about obligation.
You **must try** to be more organized.
He **has to work** on weekends.

We use *don't have to* when there is no obligation.
We **don't have to wear** a school uniform.

We use *must not* to talk about prohibition.
You **must not use** your phone on an airplane.

> The meanings of *must* and *have to* are similar in the affirmative, but different in the negative. We use *must not* when there is prohibition. We use *don't have to* when there is no obligation.
> You **must not** tell anyone.
> (don't tell anyone: it is prohibited)
> You **don't have to** tell anyone.
> (it isn't necessary to tell anyone)

Advice: *should, ought to, had better*

We use *ought to* and *should* to give advice and make recommendations. *Ought to* is more formal.
You **ought to look** for a new job.
You **should (not) look** for a new job.

We use *had better (not)* + infinitive without *to* to give advice, make threats, or express an intention.
You'**d better go** to the doctor. (advice)
You'**d better not leave**, or I'll be angry. (threat)
I'**d better help** him. (intention)

Permission: *can, could, be allowed to*

We use *can* to talk about permission in the present.
Can I go out tonight?
You **can't come** in here without a safety helmet.

We use *be allowed to* to talk about permission in the past and future.
I **won't be allowed to** go to the party.
We **were allowed to** watch the movie.

We can use *could* to talk about general permission, or permission for repeated actions, in the past.
I **couldn't** go to the mall alone until I was 15.

> We do not use *could* to talk about permission for a specific action in the past.
> I **was allowed to** stay out late last night.
> NOT I could stay out late last night.

Language Reference

Modal perfects

might / may / could have + past participle

We use **might**, **may**, or **could have** + past participle to conclude that something was possible in the past.
He **might / may / could have stolen** the money.
She **may / might not have broken** the window.

could have + past participle

We use **could have** + past participle to suggest imagined or hypothetical possibilities in the past.
You **could have been** a lawyer.
I **couldn't have won** the race because I was unfit.

must have + past participle

We use **must have** + past participle to express a certain conclusion about the past.
Life **must have been** hard when you first arrived here.
They **must have spent** a lot of money.

can't have + past participle

We use **can't have** + past participle to conclude that something was impossible in the past.
I **can't have gotten** the job because the interview was terrible.
What a strange answer! He **can't have understood** the question.

should have + past participle

We use **should have** + past participle to give an opinion about past actions, even though it is now too late to change them.
He **should have asked** for help, but he didn't.
I **should have helped** him, but I didn't.

shouldn't have + past participle

We use **shouldn't have** + past participle to express regret or criticism about past events.
I feel sick. I **shouldn't have eaten** all that pie!
She **shouldn't have been** so inflexible.

Easily-confused words

It is easy to confuse words that have similar meanings, sounds, or spellings. Here are some common examples.
- *borrow* and *lend*
  Can I **borrow** some money from you?
  = Can you **lend** me some money?
- *earn* and *win*
  He **earned** $100 working in the store yesterday.
  He **won** $100 in a competition yesterday.
- *look*, *watch*, and *see*
  Look at this photograph!
  (look = pay attention to something you can see)
  I **watched** him cross the road.
  (watch = follow something with your eyes)
  Can you **see** that man? He's waving at us!
  (see = notice something because it is visible)
- *lose* and *miss*
  Here's the key. Please **don't lose** it!
  If we're late, we'**ll miss** the train.
- *remember* and *remind*
  I must **remember** to record that movie.
  (= I must not forget.)
  Please **remind** me to record that movie. (= Please tell me to record that movie, because I might forget.)
- *say* and *tell*
  He **said** he was sorry.
  He **told** me he was sorry.

Negative prefixes

We can add a prefix to many adjectives, to make new adjectives with the opposite meaning. There are no rules, so you will need to use a dictionary. Here are some guidelines which will help in many cases:
- *un-* is the most common prefix used to make opposites.
- We use *in-* before words with a Latin origin.
- We use *im-* before words beginning with m or p.
- We use *il-* before words beginning with l.
- We use *ir-* before words beginning with r.
- We use *dis-* before adjectives and a few verbs.

un-	
friendly	**un**friendly
successful	**un**successful
in-	
flexible	**in**flexible
sufficient	**in**sufficient
im-	
polite	**im**polite
mature	**im**mature
il-	
logical	**il**logical
legal	**il**legal
ir-	
resistible	**ir**resistible
responsible	**ir**responsible
dis-	
honest	**dis**honest
obedient	**dis**obedient

Unit 3

Past perfect

Structure

We form the past perfect with **had** and the past participle.

Affirmative		
I/he/she/it/we/you/they	+ **had** (= **'d**)	+ past participle

He **had eaten**.
They **had forgotten**.

Negative		
I/he/she/it/we/you/they	+ **had not** (= **hadn't**)	+ past participle

I **hadn't asked** him.
They **hadn't seen** the movie.

Interrogative		
Had	+ I/he/she/it/we/you/they	+ past participle ?

Had you **invited** her?
Had she **played** soccer before?

Use

We use the past perfect:
- when we are already talking about the past, and we want to refer to earlier actions or situations.
  I**'d seen** the movie before I read the book.
  ```
        I saw           I read
        the movie       the book
  The past ─────┼──────────┼──────────► Now
  ```
- to talk about actions or situations which happened before a specific moment in the past.
  By the time he was 16, Rafael **had scored** 50 goals for his club.
  I**'d never failed** an exam before that one.
- with the expression *it was the first / second / third time (that)*.
  It was the third time (that) the team **had won** the competition.
- with the time expressions *by*, *before*, *after*, *when*, *as soon as*, and *until*, for example, in a narrative to indicate a sequence of events. Note that we use the past perfect for the earlier action.
  By the end of his vacation in New York, Jorge **had seen** all the tourist attractions.
  (Jorge saw all the tourist attractions, then his vacation ended)
  The game **had begun** before we arrived.
  (The game began, then we arrived)

After she**'d finished** her homework, Ana went to the gym.
= When she**'d finished** her homework, Ana went to the gym.
= As soon as she**'d finished** her homework, Ana went to the gym.
= Ana didn't go to the gym until she**'d finished** her homework.
(Ana finished her homework, then she went to the gym)

Simple past and past perfect

Contrast

We often use the simple past and the past perfect together in narrative sequences.
- We use the simple past to talk about finished actions and events in the past.
  I **arrived** at the station at 7:30.
- We use the past perfect when we are talking about the past, and we want to add information about an action that happened before. We use the simple past for the more recent action, and the past perfect to refer back to the earlier action.
  I **arrived** at the station at 7:30, but the train **had already left**. (the train left the station, then I arrived at the station)
- When we are narrating a sequence of past actions in chronological order, we use the simple past, NOT the past perfect.
  He **arrived** at the station, then he **bought** his ticket. After that, he **had** a coffee, and **waited** for his train.
  NOT ~~He had arrived at the station, then he bought his ticket.~~
- With the time expressions *after*, *before*, and *when*, we can use the simple past OR the past perfect to describe the earlier action.
  When he**'d arrived** at the station, he bought his ticket. OR When he **arrived** at the station, he bought his ticket.

Language Reference 3

too / not ... enough

Structure

too + adjective / adverb (+ *to* + infinitive)
She's feeling **too sick to eat**.
I'm not ready yet. You're **too early**!

(not) + adjective / adverb + *enough* (+ *to* + infinitive)
He can't reach the table. He is**n't tall enough**.
We're **not old enough to drive**.

Use

- We can use *too* + adjective / adverb to say that a person or thing has an excess of a particular quality.
  After the operation, I was **too weak** to walk.
  We couldn't catch her. She was running **too quickly**.
- We use *(not) enough* + adjective / adverb to say that a person or thing has sufficient, or insufficient, of a particular quality.
  She's **not fit enough** to play tennis professionally.

> When we use a verb after *too* or *(not) ... enough*, we must use an infinitive with *to*, not a gerund.
> He was too tired **to walk** any further.
> NOT He was too tired walking any further.

> Note that *too* does not mean the same as *very*. When we use *too* + adjective, we are implying that there is a problem, or a limitation. When we use *very* + adjective, we are simply stating a fact or observation.
> She's **very short**. (it's an observation; it isn't necessarily a good thing or a bad thing)
> She can't reach the bookshelf because she's **too short**. (it's a problem)

Noun suffixes (1)

We can add suffixes to many verbs to make nouns. Be careful: sometimes the spelling changes.

verb + *-ment*	
advertise	advertise**ment**
agree	agree**ment**
verb + *-ation*	
explain	explan**ation** (NOT ~~explaination~~)
invite	invit**ation** (NOT ~~inviteation~~)
verb + *-ence*	
prefer	prefer**ence**
differ	differ**ence**
verb + *-ion*	
direct	direct**ion**
promote	promot**ion**
verb + *-ance*	
appear	appear**ance**
endure	endur**ance** (NOT ~~endureance~~)

Unit 4

Relative pronouns

who, that, which, when, where, whose

We use relative pronouns to add a new clause (the relative clause) to a sentence. The relative pronoun refers to the noun before it.
That's the man. ➜ That's **the man who** works at the music store.

- We use **who** and **that** to refer to people.
  She's the woman **who / that** wrote this book.
- When the person is the object of the sentence, we can use **whom**, but only in very formal language.
  That's the woman **whom** I saw. (very formal)
  That's the woman **who / that** I saw. (informal)
- We use **which** and **that** to refer to things.
  This is the magazine **which / that** I bought.
  This is the song **which / that** I like the most.
- We use **when** to refer to time.
  2009 was the year **when** he released his first album.
- We use **where** to refer to spaces and places.
  This is the town **where** I was born.
  The club **where** they're performing is very small.
- We use **whose** to refer to possession.
  He's a composer **whose** music is world-famous.

> Don't confuse **who's** and **whose** in relative clauses.
> **Whose** is a relative pronoun, and it refers to possession.
> They're the children **whose** mother is a famous jazz singer.
> **Who's** is the contracted form of **who is** or **who has**.
> We spoke to the person **who's** (= who is) organizing the talent show.
> That's the drummer **who's** (= who has) joined the band.

that

- We can use **that** instead of **who** or **which** in relative clauses.
  He's the man **that** (= who) we met at the studio.
  Here's the guitar **that** (= which) I bought last week.
- It is very common in English to use **that** after *something, anything, everything, nothing, all,* and superlatives.
  Here's **something that** you should see.
  Do you have **anything that** you want to sell?
  That was **the worst performance that** I've ever seen!

Defining relative clauses

Use

Defining relative clauses give essential information about the noun. Without the relative clause, the sentence would be incomplete and would not make sense.
She's the woman.

This sentence is incomplete. It needs a defining relative clause.
   She's the woman. ➜ She's the woman **who wrote this song**.
   It's an animal. ➜ It's an animal **that lives in the desert**.

Omission of relative pronouns

We can omit the relative pronoun in defining relative clauses, if it is the object of the relative clause. If a relative pronoun is followed by another subject + verb, it is probably the object of a relative clause.
That's the book **(that / which)** she gave me.
He's the boy **(that / who)** I saw at the concert.

We often omit the relative pronouns **who**, **which**, **that**, and **when**, especially in spoken English.

We cannot omit the relative pronoun if it is the subject of the sentence.
That's the book **(that / which)** Felipe read last week.
(Felipe read the book ➜ *the book* = the object, and *Felipe* = the subject.)
BUT That's the book **that / which** explains the theory of relativity.
(The book explains the theory ➜ *the book* = the subject.)

> We can never omit the relative pronoun **whose**.
> This is the man **whose** car broke down.
> NOT ~~This is the man's car broke down.~~

Prepositions with relative clauses

If we use a phrasal verb in the relative clause, we usually put the preposition at the end, but before a time expression.
This is the venue that we told you **about**.
Is that the girl who you spoke **to** yesterday?

Language Reference

Gerunds and infinitives (1)

- After some verbs, including *enjoy, don't mind, dislike, can't stand, finish, imagine, give up, go, suggest, can't help,* and *practice*, we must use a gerund (*-ing* form).
  Diego **has gone swimming**.
  Sara **doesn't mind practicing** the piano.
  I **practice singing** every day.
- After some verbs, including *want, agree, need, would like, hope, promise, refuse, expect, try, decide, learn, plan, intend,* and *seem*, we must use *to* + infinitive.
  Sara **hopes to go** to the US next year.
  We **need to find** a new guitarist.
  I always **seem to get** it wrong.
- After the verbs *like, love, hate, begin, start, continue,* and *prefer*, we can use a gerund OR *to* + infinitive.
  I **like listening** to music.
  = I **like to listen** to music.
  He **loves walking** in the mountains.
  = He **loves to walk** in the mountains.
  The band **began playing** at 8 p.m.
  = The band **began to play** at 8 p.m.

Verbs		Followed by …
admit	finish	gerund (*-ing* form) only
avoid	give up	
can't help	imagine	
can't imagine	mention	
can't stand	miss	
consider	practice	
dislike	report	
don't mind	suggest	
enjoy		
afford	need	*to* + infinitive only
agree	plan	
arrange	pretend	
ask	promise	
choose	refuse	
decide	seem	
expect	tempt	
hope	try	
intend	want	
learn	would like	
manage		
begin	love	gerund OR *to* + infinitive
continue	prefer	
hate	start	
like		

Some verbs can be followed by a gerund or *to* + infinitive, but there is a change in meaning. The most common are: *regret, remember, forget,* and *stop*.

- *regret* + gerund refers to the past.
  I **regret giving up** the piano. (I regret now that in the past I gave up the piano)
- *regret to* + infinitive is used to make formal announcements of bad news.
  We **regret to inform** you of the cancelation of the flight to Washington.
- *remember* + gerund refers to something that happened before the point of remembering.
  I **remember seeing** her yesterday.
  (I remember now that I saw her yesterday)
- *remember* + *to* + infinitive refers to something that happened after the point of remembering.
  I **remembered to reserve** a table. (I remembered first, and then I reserved a table)
- *forget* + gerund refers to something that happened before the point of forgetting.
  I'll never **forget meeting** you. (I've met you; in the future, I'll never forget it)
- *forget* + *to* + infinitive refers to something that happened after the point of forgetting.
  We **forgot to watch** the movie. (We forgot, and then we didn't watch the movie)
- *stop* + gerund means "to end an action".
  I **stopped smoking**.
- *stop* + *to* + infinitive means "to interrupt one action with another action".
  I **stopped to buy** some water. (I interrupted my journey to buy some water)

Noun suffixes (2)

We can add suffixes to many nouns or verbs to make nouns which describe what people do.

noun + *-ist*	
guita**r**	guita**rist**
science	scient**ist**

noun + *-ian*	
magic	magic**ian**
politics	politic**ian**

verb + *-er*	
sing	sing**er**
manage	manag**er**

verb + *-or*	
act	act**or**
invent	invent**or**

Unit 5

Non-defining relative clauses

Non-defining relative clauses give extra information about the noun, but the information is not essential. It is similar to a parenthesis. If we remove the relative clause, the sentence still makes sense.
My uncle is going to Florida next week.

This sentence is already complete, but we can add extra information to it, in a non-defining relative clause.
My uncle, **who rarely leaves his village**, is going to Florida next week.
(The relative clause gives us extra information about my uncle.)
I stayed at the hotel, **which was very expensive**.
(The relative clause gives us extra information about the hotel.)

We cannot omit the relative pronoun from a non-defining relative clause.
Cathy, **who works in a supermarket**, is 23 years old.
NOT Cathy, works in a supermarket, is 23 years old.
My computer, **which I bought last year**, is very fast.
NOT My computer, I bought last year, is very fast.

We always use commas to separate the non-defining clause from the rest of the sentence.
The book**,** which describes life in an Amish community**,** is very interesting.
He's never drunk alcohol, which is forbidden by his religion.

We can combine two simple sentences with a non-defining relative clause.
My friend is called Matthew. He's an actor.
➔ My friend, **who's an actor**, is called Matthew.
OR
My friend, who's **called Matthew**, is an actor.

> We never use *that* in a non-defining relative clause. We always use *who* or *which*.
> These shoes, **which** I wear every day, belonged to my father.
> NOT These shoes, that I wear every day, belonged to my father.
> My sister, **who** lives in Vitoria, is a dancer.
> NOT My sister, that lives in Vitoria, is a dancer.

Special expressions with defining relative clauses

Sometimes, non-defining relative clauses can be introduced by a phrase + a relative pronoun. Here are some of the most common phrases:

all of which / whom, any of which / whom, both of which / whom, few of which / whom, many of which / whom, most of which / whom, none of which / whom.

My brothers, **both of whom** are older than me, have a lot of freedom.
(both of my brothers are older than me, and they have a lot of freedom)
Sara owns over 100 pairs of shoes, **most of which** she has never worn.
(Sara owns over 100 pairs of shows, **few of which** she has ever worn)

Language Reference

Gerunds and infinitives (2)

We can use a gerund:
- as the subject or object of a sentence.
  Running is exhausting!
  Smoking is not allowed.
  My favorite hobby is **reading**.
- after a preposition.
  Vera stepped into the road **without looking**.
  NOT ... without to look.
  Thank you **for helping** me.
- after *by* or *without* to explain how somebody does something.
  She learned a lot **by talking** with other people.
  We followed the rules **without questioning** them.

> We can put objects after gerunds.
> **Eating vegetables** is good for you.
> NOT Eating vegetables are good for you. ("eating" is the subject, and it is a singular noun)
> **Visiting Paris** was an amazing experience.
>
> We can use adjectives and possessive pronouns before gerunds.
> **Gentle swimming** is great exercise.
> That was very **dangerous driving**.
> My mother always criticizes **my cooking**.

We can use *to* + infinitive:
- to express purpose, to explain why somebody does something.
  He enrolled in a course **to improve** his English.
  She spoke slowly **to make sure** we understood.
- after an adjective.
  It's too **hot to wear** a hat.
  The discussion wasn't **easy to follow**.

Prefixes

We can add a prefix to many verbs and adjectives to modify their meaning.

re- ("do again")	
arrange	**re**arrange
consider	**re**consider
mis- ("do wrongly")	
hear	**mis**hear
understand	**mis**understand
over- ("too much")	
cook	**over**cook
react	**over**react
self- ("for, of, to, or by yourself")	
sufficient	**self**-sufficient
disciplined	**self**-disciplined
non- ("not")	
smoking	**non**-smoking
conformist	**non**-conformist
inter- ("between")	
active	**inter**active
national	**inter**national

Unit 6

The passive (1)

Structure

We form the passive voice with **be** + past participle.
We use **be** in the same tense that we would use in the active sentence.

Tense	Active	Passive
Simple present	takes	is taken
Simple past	took	was taken
Present continuous	is taking	is being taken
Past continuous	was taking	was being taken

They choose a different location for each episode.
→ A different location **is chosen** for each episode.
They broadcast the show on TV last fall.
→ The show **was broadcast** on TV last fall.
They are filming some scenes in New York.
→ Some scenes **are being filmed** in New York.
People were taking photos of the cast.
→ Photos **were being taken** of the cast.

When we change an active sentence to a passive sentence, the object of the active sentence becomes the subject of the passive sentence.

Active: John Logie Baird invented the TV.
           subject   verb   object

Passive: The TV was invented by John Logie Baird.
           subject   verb   agent

> In informal, spoken English, we sometimes make passives with **get** instead of **be**.
> I **get paid** at the end of the month.
> MORE COMMON THAN I **am paid** at the end of the month.
> She **got seen** by the doctor immediately.
>
> We usually use **get** instead of **be** in the passive phrases **get married** and **get arrested**.
> Terry and Ana **got married** in 2005.
> MORE COMMON THAN Terry and Ana **were married** in 2005.

Use

When we want to say what a person or thing does, we use an active verb. When we want to say what happens to a person or thing, we use a passive verb.
We **bought** a new TV last week. (it is important to say who bought a new TV)
Thousands of new TVs **are bought** every day. (it is not important to say who buys them)

We use the passive voice:
- to emphasize the action (the verb), more than the person who did the action.
  The TV station is showing the game at 7 p.m.
  → The game **is being shown** at 7 p.m.
- when we don't know who did the action, or when it is not important who did it.
  Somebody has stolen my camera!
  → My camera **has been stolen**!
- to put the most important idea at the beginning of the sentence.
  Industrialization is destroying the rainforests.
  → The rainforests **are being destroyed** by industrialization.
- when we want to continue talking about the same subject in a new sentence, and we don't want to introduce a new subject.
  Chili peppers are an important ingredient in the Mexican diet. They **are used** in many traditional dishes.
  BETTER THAN People use them ...

> Some verbs do not have a passive form. These include intransitive verbs (action verbs which do not take an object), such as **die**, **sleep**, and **swim**.
> We swam.
> NOT We were swum.

Language Reference 6

-ed and -ing adjectives

We can add the suffixes -ed and -ing to some verbs, to form adjectives which describe feelings.

- Adjectives which end in -ed describe how a person feels.
  There's nothing to do. I'm **bored**. (I'm talking about the way I feel)
- Adjectives which end in -ing describe the cause of a feeling.
  This movie is really **boring**. (I'm talking about the movie)

These are some common -ed and -ing adjectives.

Verb	Adjectives	Examples
amaze	amaz**ed**	I was **amazed** at his strength.
	amaz**ing**	His strength was **amazing**.
amuse	amus**ed**	His jokes were funny and we were **amused**.
	amus**ing**	His jokes were **amusing**.
bore	bor**ed**	I'm **bored**.
	bor**ing**	This movie is **boring**.
disappoint	disappoint**ed**	He was **disappointed** with his results.
	disappoint**ing**	His results were **disappointing**.
embarrass	embarrass**ed**	She was **embarrassed** because she did badly.
	embarrass**ing**	Her performance was **embarrassing**.
excite	excit**ed**	Diego was **excited** to hear the news.
	excit**ing**	The news was **exciting**.
exhaust	exhaust**ed**	Carlos was **exhausted** after the race.
	exhaust**ing**	The race was **exhausting**.
frighten	frighten**ed**	They were **frightened** by a loud noise.
	frighten**ing**	The noise was **frightening**.
interest	interest**ed**	She's **interested** in biology.
	interest**ing**	She thinks biology is **interesting**.
intrigue	intrigu**ed**	How will the story finish? I'm **intrigued**.
	intrigu**ing**	This story is **intriguing**.
move	mov**ed**	The last episode was very sad. Everyone was **moved**.
	mov**ing**	The last episode was **moving**.

have / get something done

Structure

have / get (any tense) + object + past participle
The actors **are having** their make-up **done**.
He **had** his costume **cleaned**.

Use

- We use *have something done* (causative) to talk about actions which we do not do ourselves. We ask or pay another person to do them for us.
  I **had** my apartment **decorated**. (I didn't decorate it myself: I paid someone to decorate it)
- We can also use *get something done*. It has the same meaning as *have something done*, but it is more informal.
  I **got** my eyes **tested**.
  They**'re getting** their hair **cut**.
- If it is important to name the person who does the action (the "agent", see page 76), we can use *by*.
  We had photos taken **by a professional photographer**.

If somebody else does the action for us, we don't use a regular active structure.
I **had** my hair **cut**.
NOT I cut my hair.

Two structures with a similar meaning to *have / get something done* are:

have somebody do something
I **had** a photographer **take** some photos.

get somebody to do something
I **got** a photographer **to take** some photos.

These structures are more common than *have / get something done* if it's important to name the agent.
He had the producer find a new location.
OR He got the producer to find a new location.
BETTER THAN He had a new location found by the producer.

75

Unit 7

The passive (2)

We can use a passive form of present perfect and past perfect verbs. Modal verbs also have a passive form.

Tense	Active	Passive
Present perfect	has taken	has been taken
Past perfect	had taken	had been taken
will	will take	will be taken
Modals	can take	can be taken

Someone has installed solar panels on this building.
➡ Solar panels **have been installed** on this building.
By 2005, they had constructed hundreds of wind turbines.
➡ By 2005, hundreds of wind turbines **had been constructed**.
In the next 50 years, we will deplete our reserves of oil.
➡ In the next 50 years, our reserves of oil **will be depleted**.
People should recycle waste paper.
➡ Waste paper **should be recycled**.

In a passive sentence, we use *by* before the object. We call the object of a passive sentence the "agent".
Pollution has cause serious problems.
➡ Serious problems have been caused **by** pollution.
(pollution is the agent)

We omit *by* + agent:
- when the agent is unknown.
  The vegetables were grown in Africa. (I don't know who grew them)
- when the agent is obvious, or when it is not important to mention the agent.
  New laws will be introduced. (it is obvious that the government will introduce them)
- if we do not want to name the agent.
  The window was broken while we were playing soccer. (the speaker does not want to say who broke the window)

It is not always possible to omit *by* + agent. Some sentences need an agent because it is important information.
My grandfather had planted the trees.
➡ The trees had been planted **by my grandfather**.
Wind power can generate electricity.
➡ Electricity can be generated **by wind power**.

Transformations: active ➡ passive

We can use the following five steps to change an active sentence into a passive sentence.
Active: They have insulated the buildings.
1 Identify the object of the active sentence:
   the buildings
2 Put it at the beginning of the passive sentence.
   It is now the subject: *The buildings*
3 Identify the tense of the active sentence: *have insulated* = present perfect
4 Use the same tense of the verb *be*. Then add the past participle of the main verb: *have been insulated*
5 Decide if you need to use *by* + the agent (*they*):
Passive: The buildings have been insulated.
NOT ~~The buildings have been insulated by them.~~
(We do not know who "they" are.)

Transformations: passive ➡ active

To change a passive sentence into an active one, follow the steps above, but in reverse. It might be necessary to invent a subject.
Passive: They were being followed.
(Who was following them? We don't know, so we have to say "someone" in the active sentence.)
➡ **Active:** Someone was following them.
Passive: Food is imported by supermarkets.
➡ **Active:** Supermarkets import food.

The passive with reporting verbs

We can use the passive to report feelings and beliefs. The agent is only included if it is necessary. Reporting verbs commonly used in the passive include: *accept*, *believe*, *expect*, *hope*, *know*, *say*, *think*, *understand*.

We can use passive reporting verbs in two ways:
- subject + passive reporting verb + *to* + infinitive
  Martin **is expected** to pass the test.
  The president **is believed** to be meeting the prime minister tomorrow.
- *it* + passive reporting verb + *that*
  It is expected that Martin will pass the test.
  It's believed that the president will meet the prime minister tomorrow.

either ... or and *neither ... nor*

When we talk about a situation where there are two possibilities, we can use *either ... or* or *neither ... nor*.

	Possibility A	Possibility B
	✓	✗
either ... or	✗	✓
neither ... nor	✗	✗

When we talk about a choice between two possibilities, we normally use *or*.
You can have tea **or** coffee.

We can emphasize *or* by using *either ... or*. This makes it clear that you can only choose one of the two possibilities.
You can have **either** tea **or** coffee. (you can have tea, or you can have coffee, but you can't have both)

When we talk about a situation where there are two possibilities, but we are not allowed to choose either one, we use *neither ... nor*.

Language Reference

You can have **neither** tea **nor** coffee. (you can't have tea and you can't have coffee)

Neither ... nor is formal. It is more common to use *not ... or*, or *not ... and not ... either*.
You can't have tea **or** coffee.
OR You can't have tea **and** you can't have coffee **either**.

Prefixes and suffixes: summary

We can add prefixes to many nouns, adjectives, and verbs to modify their meaning. The following chart lists the prefixes that we use to make opposites.

noun, verb, or adjective	opposite meaning
happy	**un**happy
convenient	**in**convenient
mobilize	**im**mobilize
logical	**il**logical
replaceable	**ir**replaceable
belief	**dis**belief
stick	**non**-stick

The following chart lists some of the prefixes that we use to modify the meaning of nouns, adjectives and verbs in other ways.

noun, verb, or adjective	modified meaning
create	**re**create (= create again)
hear	**mis**hear (= hear wrongly)
stay	**over**stay (= stay too long)
achieve	**under**achieve (= not achieve enough)
taught	**self**-taught (= taught by yourself)

We can add the suffixes *-ist* and *-ian* to the name of a musical instrument or academic subject to make a new noun to describe a person. See page 71 for more information.

noun	noun describing a person
piano	pian**ist**
biology	biolog**ist**
music	music**ian**

We can add suffixes to many nouns and verbs to make them into different parts of speech.

- We can add the suffixes *-ance*, *-ence*, *-ation*, *-ion*, *-er*, *-or*, *-ment*, *-ent*, and *-ant* to some verbs to make nouns. See page 69 for more information.

verb	noun
appear	appear**ance**
prefer	prefer**ence**
explore	explor**ation**
direct	direct**ion**
sing	sing**er**
act	act**or**
move	move**ment**

We can add the suffixes *-ive*, *-able*, *-ible*, *-ed*, and *-ing* to some verbs to make adjectives.

verb	adjective
attract	attract**ive**
sustain	sustain**able**
resist	resist**ible**
tire	tir**ed** / tir**ing**

- We can add the suffixes *-y*, *-al*, *-ful*, *-less*, *-ous*, *-ive*, *-ic*, and *-ish* to some nouns to make adjectives.

noun	adjective
hunger	hungr**y**
music	music**al**
help	help**ful**
care	care**less**
fame	fam**ous**
expense	expens**ive**
athlete	athlet**ic**
self	self**ish**

Unit 8

Reported speech

Structure

We use reported speech to report what another person has said, without saying their exact words.
"I'm happy with my life," he said.
→ He said that he was happy with his life.

In formal language, we begin the reported speech clause with *that*. In informal language, we can omit *that*.
"I don't want to go to prison," said the girl.
→ The girl said (that) she didn't want to go to prison.

Notice that speech marks ("…") are not used in reported speech.

Reported statements: tense changes

When we convert direct speech into reported speech, we change the tense of the main verb by putting it one step further into the past.
"I **will remember** you," she said.
→ She said she **would remember** me.

Direct speech	→	Reported speech
Simple present I wait	→	Simple past I waited
Present continuous I am waiting	→	Past continuous I was waiting
Present perfect I have waited	→	Past perfect I had waited
Simple past I waited	→	Past perfect I had waited
Past perfect I had waited	→	Past perfect I had waited
will I will wait	→	would I would wait
can I can wait	→	could I could wait
must I must wait	→	had to I had to wait

We don't change the past perfect in reported speech.
"I **hadn't been** to Rio de Janeiro before I came here to work," he said.
→ He said he **hadn't been** to Rio de Janeiro before he came here to work.

Most modal verbs (for example, *should*, *could*, *would*, *might*, *ought to*) do not change.
"You **should** apologize to him."
→ She said that I **should** apologize to him.
"I **could** help you."
→ He said that he **could** help me.
BUT "I **can** lend you some money."
→ He said that he **could** lend me some money.

Reported questions

Reported questions have a different word order from direct questions. They have the same word order as an affirmative sentence.

- verb + subject (direct question)
  → subject + verb (reported question)
  "Where is the youth center?" she asked.
  → She asked (me) where the youth center was.
  NOT She asked me where was the youth center.

If a direct question uses question words, for example, *who*, *why*, *when*, *how*, *what*, we repeat the question word in the reported question.
"**Why** did you skip school?" he asked her.
→ He asked her **why** she had skipped school.
"**When** are you leaving?" she asked me.
→ She asked me **when** I was leaving.

If a direct question does not use question words (*who*, *why*, *when*, *how*, *what*), we use *if* or *whether* in the reported question.
"Are you in trouble?" he asked her.
→ He asked her **if / whether** she was in trouble.
"Did they commit the crime?" she asked him.
→ She asked him **if / whether** they had committed the crime.

Reported orders and requests

In direct speech, we use the imperative to give orders and make requests. In reported speech, we use the following structures:

- **orders:** subject + verb + object + *to* + infinitive
  "Stay away!" he said to them.
  → He **ordered them** to stay away.
  "Be careful!" she told him.
  → She **told him** to be careful.
- **requests:** subject + *ask* + object + *to* + infinitive
  "Can you help me?" the girl asked me.
  → The girl **asked me to help** her.

If we want to make a negative command in reported speech, we put *not* before *to* + infinitive:

- subject + verb + object + *not* + *to* + infinitive
  "Don't be silly!"
  → He told her **not to be silly**.
  "Don't argue!"
  → He told us **not to argue**.

These are some of the verbs we can use to give commands in reported speech: *advise*, *ask*, *encourage*, *order*, *remind*, *tell*, *warn*.
"Talk to a therapist."
→ She **advised** me to talk to a therapist.
"Don't break the law."
→ He **warned** her not to break the law.

Language Reference 8

Reported suggestions

We use the reporting verb *suggest* in reported suggestions. We can use the verb *suggest* in two different ways:
- subject + *suggest* + gerund
  "Let's go by bus."
  → He suggested **going** by bus.
  "Why don't we sing a song?"
  → She suggested **singing** a song.
- subject + *suggest that* + present subjunctive
  "Let's go by bus."
  → He suggested **that we go** by bus.
  BUT "You should go by bus."
  → I suggested **that he go** by bus.
  NOT I suggested **that he goes** by bus.

> The present subjunctive is similar to the simple present, BUT the third person singular (*he / she / it*) form does NOT end in *-(e)s*.
> Simple present   Present subjunctive
> I/You/We/They work. I/You/We/They work.
> He/She/It work**s**.   He/She/It work.
> I/You/We/They go.   I/You/We/They go.
> He/She/It go**es**.   He/She/It go.

Reported statements: other changes

When we change direct speech into reported speech:
- pronouns usually change.
  "I'm supporting **you**," she said.
  → She said that **she** was supporting **me**.
  "We've told **you** everything," they said.
  → They said that **they** had told **me** everything.
  "**You're my** best friend," she said.
  → She said that **I** was **her** best friend.
- expressions of time and place usually change.

Direct speech	→	Reported speech
here	→	there
this	→	that
these	→	those
now	→	then
today	→	that day
tonight	→	that night
tomorrow	→	the next OR following day
next week / month / year	→	the next OR following week / month / year
yesterday	→	the day before OR the previous day
last night / week / month / year	→	the night / week / month / year before OR the previous night / week / month / year

"We'll meet **here tomorrow**," she said.
→ She said that they would meet **there the next day**.
"I'm going to buy **these now**," he said.
→ He said he was going to buy **those then**.

- most modal verbs (for example, *should*, *could*, *would*, *might*, *ought to*) do not change.
  "The police **might** arrest him," she said.
  → She said that the police **might** arrest him.
  "I **couldn't** solve the problem," he said.
  → He said that he **couldn't** solve the problem.
  BUT "I **can** show you the way," he said
  → He said that he **could** show me the way.

Reporting verbs

In reported speech, we can use many different verbs. The chart below shows some common reporting verbs together with the correct structure.

Reporting verb	Structure	Example
add, admit, agree, announce, declare, explain, insist, recall, recommend, reply, report, reveal, say, suggest, tell	verb + (*that*)	He **added (that)** he was sorry.
advise, ask, invite, order, remind, tell	verb + object + *to* + infinitive	She **advised me to call** the police.
agree, decide, offer, promise, refuse, threaten	verb + *to* + infinitive	She **agreed to help**.
apologize for, deny, regret, suggest	verb + gerund	He **apologized for being** rude.

Word list

Starter unit

Nouns
chore
date
relationship

Verbs and verb phrases
ask (someone) out
break up (with)
cancel
fall for
get over
go out (with)
introduce
keep in touch (with)
let (someone) down
pick

Adjectives
cute
good-looking
gorgeous
nervous
shy
upset

Adverb phrase
right away

Collocations with do
do (your) best
do chores
do the dishes
do an exercise
do someone a favor
do (your) hair
do homework
do a job
do nothing
do well

Collocations with make
make an arrangement
make a change
make a decision
make a difference
make an effort
make friends
make an impression
make a mistake
make plans
make a suggestion

Unit 1

Nouns
apartment
bill
closet
electricity
energy
furniture
heat
heater
possession
solar panels
stool
storage
workshop

Verbs and verb phrases
afford
attend
cater to
damage
downsize
heat
maintain
move in
put together
realize
take off

Adjectives
affordable
bruised
charming
chilly
comfortable
contemporary
convenient
cozy
cramped
eco-friendly
expensive
fresh
inconvenient
large
old-fashioned
pleasant
satisfying
spacious
uninviting
unpleasant
unsatisfied
warm

Adverbs
lately
nonstop
recently
successfully

Unit 2

Nouns
agriculture
custom
employee
exploration
fortune
infrastructure
migrant
newcomer
slump
unemployment
vacancy

Verbs and verb phrases
account for
earn a living
leave behind
remind
seek
take up
think over
trust

Adjectives
adaptable
booming
considerate
current
dependable
disheartened
(un)employed
energetic
(in)flexible
hard-working
kind
(il)legal
(il)logical
(dis)obedient
(dis)organized
mere
outgoing
particular
(im)polite
reliable
(ir)replaceable
(ir)resistible
sociable
(un)successful
(in)sufficient
terrific
vast

Adverb
rapidly

Unit 3

Nouns
amusement
appearance
determination
endorsement
endurance
explanation
imitation
ingenuity
opponent
preference
promotion
reduction
salary
tolerance
try-out

Verbs and verb phrases
appoint
bring up
close down
prove
score a goal
see off
succeed
take on

Adjectives
cute
formidable
good-looking
huge
overweight
petite
powerful
ruthless
skilful
slender
slim
strong
tiny
ugly
weak

Unit 4

Nouns
bassist
confidence
cue
director
drummer
electrician
gig
guitarist
inventor
ladder
legend
magazine
magician
manager
politician
receptionist

Language Reference

talent show
tour
tutor
venue

Verbs and verb phrases
compose
download
look up to
perform
practice
promote
record
rehearse
release
settle down
sign
spot
stand out
take part (in)
take place
wind down

Adjectives
glamorous
obvious

Adverb
generally

Unit 5
Nouns
coast
community
crime
crowd
divorce
dress code
misunderstanding
ocean
overcrowding
parent

Verbs and verb phrases
abstain (from)
accept
allow
bring up
come across
discuss
experience
explore
find common ground
follow
guide
interact
mishear
observe

put (someone) off
reconsider
resume
stab
struggle
try out
worship

Adjectives
devout
forbidden
illuminating
multinational
non-conformist
self-sufficient
square
strict

Adverb
originally

Unit 6
Nouns
cast
character
cosmetic surgery
costume
critic
desert island
disability
episode
fan
location
make-up
pregnancy
producer
racism
reality show
scene
season
sitcom
stranger
topic
viewer

Verbs and verb phrases
broadcast
criticize
decorate
disregard
fall out
film
keep up with
make up
portray
praise
raise awareness
show off

Adjectives
controversial
educational
impressionable
intrigued
moved
ongoing
primetime
wealthy

Adverbs
constantly
deliberately

Unit 7
Nouns
carbon emission
congestion
construction
fossil fuel
generation
groceries
movement
pollution
renewable energy
reserve
solar panels
transportation
vegetable
waste
wind turbine

Verbs and verb phrases
allocate
anticipate
consume
cut down (on)
generate
import
install
insulate
measure
monitor
phase out
plant
recycle
reduce
require
resort to
rethink
underestimate
use up

Adjectives
communal
locally-sourced
precious

realistic
self-taught
sustainable
unnecessary

Adverb
consequently

Unit 8
Nouns
argument
assault
crowd
gang
offender
participant
prison
solution
therapist

Verbs and verb phrases
admit
announce
apologize
arrest
assign
benefit (from)
break the law
bump into
commit (a crime)
convict
cut (yourself) off
fall in with
incarcerate
lock up
offend
punish
rehabilitate
remove
sentence
serve
skip school
supervise

Adjectives
available
clear
juvenile
lenient
previous

Adverbs
approximately
dramatically

Claire Thacker
Nicholas Tims
Airton Pozo de Mattos

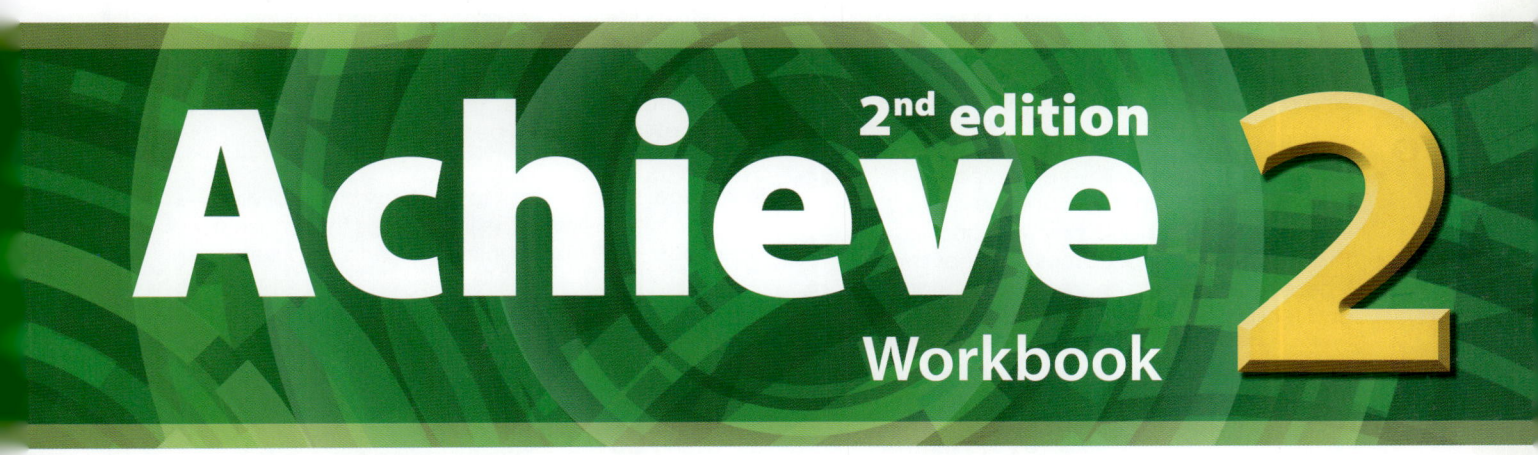

Achieve 2 — 2nd edition
Workbook

CONTENTS

Starter unit	Relationships	p84
Unit 1	Home Sweet Home	p88
Unit 2	The World of Work	p94
Unit 3	Sports Heroes	p100
Unit 4	A Career in Music	p106
Unit 5	Different Worlds	p112
Unit 6	TV Trends	p118
Unit 7	Protecting Our Planet	p124
Unit 8	Bad Behavior	p130

OXFORD UNIVERSITY PRESS

Starter

Relationships

Reading

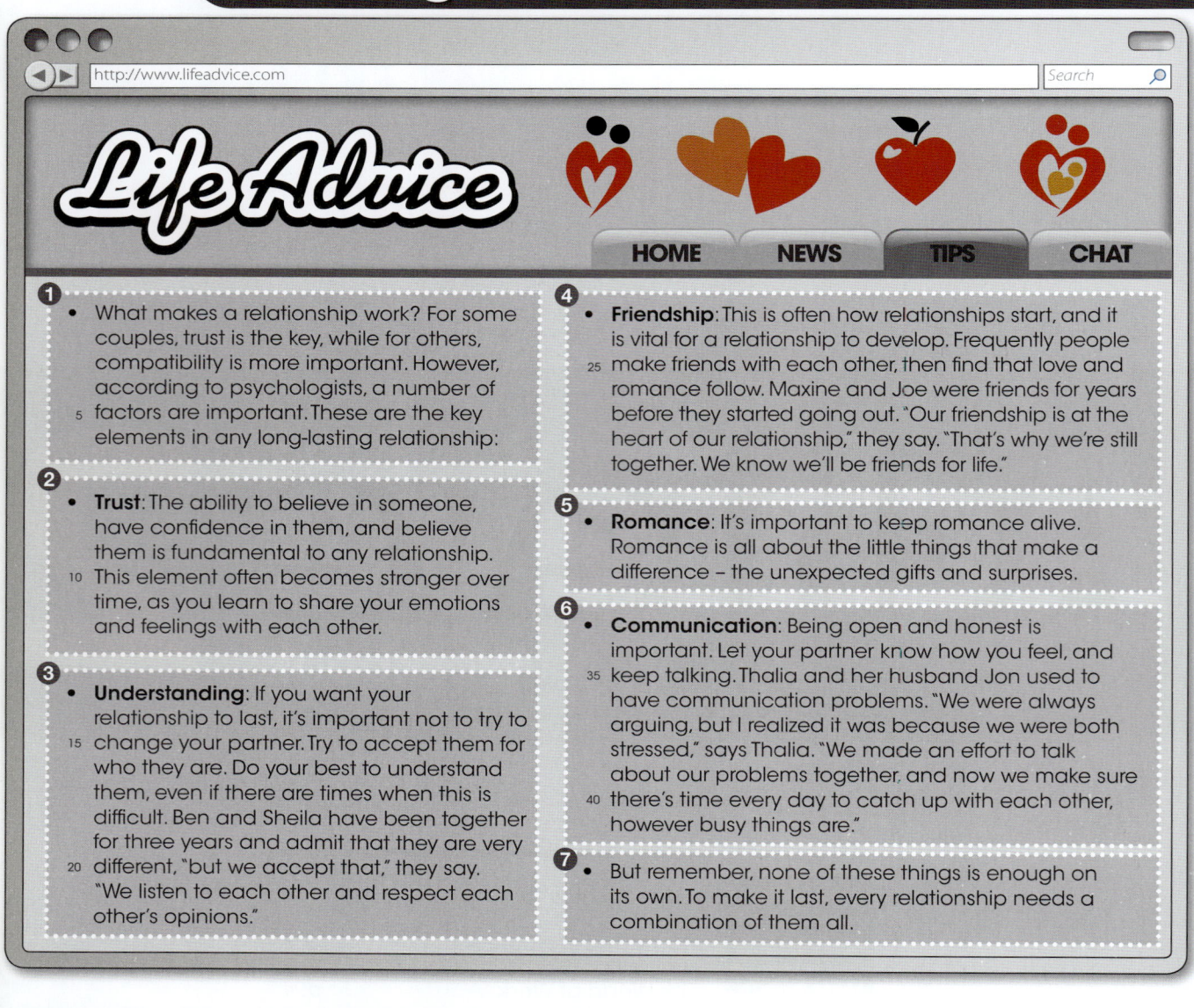

http://www.lifeadvice.com

Life Advice

HOME | NEWS | TIPS | CHAT

1 • What makes a relationship work? For some couples, trust is the key, while for others, compatibility is more important. However, according to psychologists, a number of factors are important. These are the key elements in any long-lasting relationship:

2 • **Trust**: The ability to believe in someone, have confidence in them, and believe them is fundamental to any relationship. This element often becomes stronger over time, as you learn to share your emotions and feelings with each other.

3 • **Understanding**: If you want your relationship to last, it's important not to try to change your partner. Try to accept them for who they are. Do your best to understand them, even if there are times when this is difficult. Ben and Sheila have been together for three years and admit that they are very different, "but we accept that," they say. "We listen to each other and respect each other's opinions."

4 • **Friendship**: This is often how relationships start, and it is vital for a relationship to develop. Frequently people make friends with each other, then find that love and romance follow. Maxine and Joe were friends for years before they started going out. "Our friendship is at the heart of our relationship," they say. "That's why we're still together. We know we'll be friends for life."

5 • **Romance**: It's important to keep romance alive. Romance is all about the little things that make a difference – the unexpected gifts and surprises.

6 • **Communication**: Being open and honest is important. Let your partner know how you feel, and keep talking. Thalia and her husband Jon used to have communication problems. "We were always arguing, but I realized it was because we were both stressed," says Thalia. "We made an effort to talk about our problems together, and now we make sure there's time every day to catch up with each other, however busy things are."

7 • But remember, none of these things is enough on its own. To make it last, every relationship needs a combination of them all.

---

1 Skim the advice article quickly. Choose the best title.

A Love never lasts   B Ingredients for a lasting relationship   C Together forever

2 Read the article again. Complete the sentences.

Relationships last because of _a number of factors_ .

1 During a relationship, trust can often _____.
2 To help a relationship last, it's important not to _____.
3 Couples should respect _____.
4 Relationships often begin with _____.
5 If you have communication problems, it's good to _____.

3 Read definitions 1–5. Match them with words in the article.

the ability of people to live together without problems (n), (paragraph 1) _compatibility_

1 central; forming the necessary basis of something (adj), (paragraph 2) _____
2 have a good opinion of someone or something (v), (paragraph 3) _____
3 love or the feeling of being in love (n), (paragraph 4) _____
4 too anxious and tired to be able to relax (adj), (paragraph 6) _____
5 two or more things joined together to make one (n), (paragraph 7) _____

Vocabulary

Relationships

do and make

1 Complete the chart with the words and phrases below.

a difference • an effort • an impression • friends • someone a favor • well • your best • ~~your hair~~

do	make
your hair	4 _____
1 _____	5 _____
2 _____	6 _____
3 _____	7 _____

2 Complete the dialogues with the collocations in exercise 1. Use the correct form of *do* or *make*.

A I'm really worried about my exams.
B You'll be fine. You can only _do your best_.

1 A What's the new boy in your class like?
B He's very shy. I think he's finding it difficult to _____.

2 A Can you _____ me _____ and drive me to the store?
B Sure!

3 A We're going to have to _____ to find out about college courses this term.
B You're right. Where shall we start?

4 A Why don't we do some charity work in the vacation?
B That's a great idea. We can learn new skills and _____.

5 A Imogen is taking a long time to get ready.
B Yes, she is _____ and make-up. It takes her at least an hour!

6 A I think Carolina _____ on David at the party last week.
B Yes, I know. He's still talking about her!

7 A Grandpa, did you _____ in your exams when you were at school?
B I did OK, but I had to leave school at thirteen and find a job.

Focus on phrasal verbs

3 Complete the verbs 1–6 with particles A–F.

1 ask _D_   2 go ___   3 break ___   4 let ___   5 get ___   6 fall ___
A up   B for   C down   D out   E over   F out

4 Complete the text. Use the correct form of the verbs in exercise 3.

When I _broke up_ _____ with my first boyfriend I cried for weeks. I don't think I ever (1) _____ him. When I first met him at our school prom, he looked so handsome and I (2) _____ him immediately. I think he felt the same because he (3) _____ me _____ the next day. We arranged to meet in a café after school. I couldn't believe it when he (4) _____ me _____ and forgot to come! I was pretty upset, but I forgave him. In the end, we (5) _____ for two years.

Language reference page 63

Grammar

Present tenses

1 Circle the correct alternatives.

Dina **is** / **is being** really good with other people.

1 Guess what! Leo **goes out** / **is going out** with Ruth again!
2 Samir always **wears** / **is wearing** that T-shirt on the weekend!
3 I **don't have** / **am not having** a boyfriend at the moment.
4 Hey, look! Nico **talks** / **is talking** to that girl again.
5 They **watch** / **are watching** that TV show called *Daisy of Love*.

2 Complete the dialogue. Use the correct form of the simple present or present continuous.

Sonia *Is* Ben *going out* (go out) with Ariana?
Jack No. He (1) _____ (not want) to ask her out. He's too shy!
Sonia I know she (2) _____ (not date) anyone right now.
Jack Yes, but he never (3) _____ (talk) to her on his own.
Sonia Let's invite them both to a party on the weekend.
Jack OK. Then what?
Sonia Well, I (4) _____ (not know). I (5) _____ still _____ (think) about it.

Past tenses

3 Choose the correct answers.

Dean and Carol-Ann ____ each other at school.
A weren't meeting   **B didn't meet**

1 While I ____ in the café, the waiter asked me out!
  A was sitting   B sat
2 My mom and dad ____ at a high school dance in 1971.
  A were meeting   B met
3 Lucia's very upset. Her new boyfriend ____ with her after two weeks.
  A broke up   B was breaking up
4 We ____ to the movie theater last Friday when our car broke down.
  A drove   B were driving
5 I ____ to Felipe at the party last night when my mom called me.
  A was talking   B talked

4 Complete the text with the correct forms of the verbs below. Use the simple past or the past continuous.

ask • be • know • make • meet • sit • spend • ~~think~~ • travel • visit

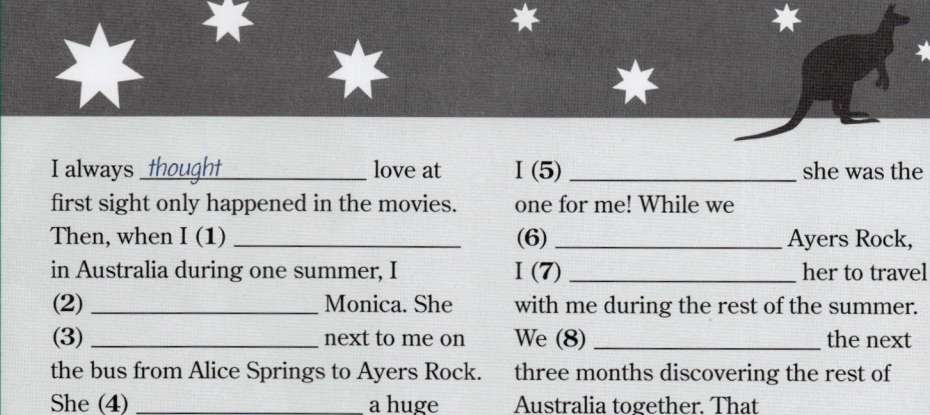

I always *thought* love at first sight only happened in the movies. Then, when I (1) _____ in Australia during one summer, I (2) _____ Monica. She (3) _____ next to me on the bus from Alice Springs to Ayers Rock. She (4) _____ a huge impression on me with her bright green eyes and gorgeous smile! I (5) _____ she was the one for me! While we (6) _____ Ayers Rock, I (7) _____ her to travel with me during the rest of the summer. We (8) _____ the next three months discovering the rest of Australia together. That (9) _____ five years ago and we are still together!

Relationships

5 Complete the conversations with the correct question word below.

Are • Did • Do • ~~What~~ • When • Where • Why

A _What_ did you do on your first date?
B We went to the movies.
1 A _____ did you meet your girlfriend?
  B At school.
2 A _____ you think Troy is good-looking?
  B Yes, he's gorgeous!
3 A _____ did you break up with Ivan?
  B Yesterday.
4 A _____ are you wearing those nice clothes?
  B Because I'm going out with my new girlfriend.
5 A _____ you still upset about Brad?
  B A little.
6 A _____ you use to go out with Betsy Marks?
  B Yes, but only for a few weeks!

Future forms

6 Circle the correct alternatives.

MESSAGES

Hi Robbie,
(**Are you going** / **Will you go**) to school dance next week? I don't think I (1) **'m going** / **'ll go** because I don't have a date. Very embarrassing!
Alex

Hey Alex,
Don't worry. It (2) **'ll be** / **'s being** a great night even without a date! I (3) **'m taking** / **'ll take** Martha so we (4) **'re meeting** / **'ll meet** you outside the hall at 8 p.m.
R

Hey Robbie,
Cool! Thanks, but I (5) **'m working** / **going to work** until 8 p.m. that night so I (6) **won't get** / **am not getting** there until 9 p.m. Is that too late?
A

Hi Alex,
It's never too late for the dance! I (7) **'ll see** / **'m seeing** you there at 9 p.m.!

7 Complete the sentences and questions. Use the correct future forms of the verbs in parentheses. More than one correct answer may be possible.

1 The weather is beautiful today. I _____ outside. (**sit**)
2 Don't worry about the argument with Paul. I'm sure he _____ you later. (**call**)
3 Shh! You _____ my little brother up. It's really late. (**wake**)
4 What _____ you _____ to Josh's party tomorrow? (**wear**)
5 What _____ you _____ after school today? Do you have band practice? (**do**)
6 Lisa has a place at college for next year. When _____ she _____? (**start**)

1 Home Sweet Home

Reading

At the heart of a community

Nearly one billion people around the world are currently living in slums, or "informal settlements". The United Nations Human Settlements Program (UNHSP) predicts that this number could double by 2030 and triple by 2050. This will put increasing pressure on these
5 settlements, which consist of cramped, low-quality buildings. There may be no easy solution to the problem of overcrowding. But at least in some slums, artists have been working with local residents to make their environments less unpleasant – and to create a sense of community pride.

10 In Rio de Janeiro, Dutch artists Dre Urhahn and Jeroen Koolhaas have been making a mark on the local landscape for several years. They first visited the slum, or favela, of Vila Cruzeiro in 2005, to make a documentary about hip-hop music. During that time, they lived in the community and soon realized that there was a big gap
15 between the perception of the favelas, and the reality. Favelas are just like any other neighborhood: a place where normal families live, where everyone has dreams, and parents want a better future for their children.

That experience had such a profound effect on them that they wanted
20 to help improve the perception of Vila Cruzeiro and its residents. And so, the Favela Painting project was born. Large-scale mural projects have transformed the area into such a visually appealing place that both foreign and local tourists have started coming to see them.

Since then, community painting projects have taken off in other
25 areas. In 2009, Urhahn and Koolhaas established the *Tudo de Cor para Santa Marta* project in another Rio favela. Local residents painted 33 old-fashioned houses in the main square in a rainbow of color. Their exteriors now look charming, bright, and colorful, and the residents learned new skills during the process. Both projects have clearly put
30 the residents' sense of community on display.

Urhahn and Koolhaas have now moved to Philadelphia in the US, and have been discussing their ideas for a major public art project, which will include a huge mural, with local residents. Watch this space …

1 Look at the photos and the title. What do you think the article is about? Skim the article and check.

2 Read the article. Choose the best alternative title for the article.

   A Painting a better future   B Design your own home   C Home is where the heart is

3 Read statements A–E. According to the article, which one is **not** true?

   A Art and design can help a community feel proud.
   B By 2030, there will be double the number of people living in slums than there are now.
   C The Dutch artists had the idea for the Favela Painting project in the US.
   D The Favela Painting project improves the buildings in a community.
   E The projects gave local people new practical skills.

Home Sweet Home   1

4 Read the lists of adjectives. According to the article, which is the best description of the Santa Marta main square now?

A expensive, modern, spacious
B inviting, pleasant, colorful
C old-fashioned, unpleasant, inconvenient
D cramped, uninviting, affordable
E cozy, modern, warm

5 Read the article again. Choose the correct answers.

1 By 2050, more and more people will …
  A be able to afford better housing.
  B travel abroad to live and work.
  C live in slums in cities.
  D want to be part of a local community.
  E want to escape city slums.

2 Favela Painting projects show how art can …
  A increase the price of housing.
  B make people feel they want to move house.
  C make slums more affordable.
  D improve the inside of homes.
  E unite members of a community

3 When Urhahn and Koolhaas were in Vila Cruzeiro, they …
  A set up a hip-hop band.
  B decided to start the Favela Painting project.
  C didn't live in the local community.
  D taught people about hip-hop music.
  E taught art to local residents.

4 Urhahn and Koolhaas wanted to …
  A transform the slums into modern houses.
  B change the slums into affordable homes.
  C design and paint a whole city.
  D ask residents to paint new houses.
  E improve the way people think about favelas.

5 Many residents benefitted from the project because …
  A they have new homes.
  B they all have new jobs.
  C they learned new skills.
  D they are still working on the project.
  E they designed their own homes.

6 Projects like this …
  A only make a difference to the buildings.
  B have no long-term benefits for a community.
  C don't improve the appearance of buildings.
  D can have a big impact on a whole community.
  E only work when the artists live in the community.

6 Find words 1–6 in the article. Match them with definitions A–F.

1 settlements (line 2) ____
2 perception (line 15) ____
3 neighborhood (line 16) ____
4 profound (line 19) ____
5 mural (line 21) ____
6 rainbow (line 27) ____

A a district or area of a town, and the people who live there
B very deep
C a curved band of different colors that appears in the sky when the sun shines through rain
D places where people establish and build their own homes
E a large picture painted on a wall
F a particular way of looking at something

7 Read the article again. Answer the questions in your own words.

1 According to the article, why will slum accommodation be a problem by 2050?
_____

2 Why did Urhahn and Koolhaas decide to start the Favela Painting project?
_____

3 How do we know that the Favela Painting project was a success? Infer from the article.
_____

Vocabulary

Adjectives: home and place

1 Find six more adjectives in the wordsearch. Then complete the sentences with the adjectives.

We stayed in a _cozy_ log cabin in the mountains last winter. It was wonderful.

1 My college dorm room last year was very _____. There was only space for a bed, a desk, and a closet.
2 It was very difficult finding an _____ apartment in the center of Buenos Aires.
3 The hotel was right next to the beach which was really _____.
4 The real estate agent told us the apartment was small, but _____.
5 My grandparents' house is very _____. They've lived there for 45 years and haven't changed anything!
6 I love _____ buildings and architecture. My favorite is the Guggenheim Museum in Bilbao.

C	A	B	C	T	D	Z	C	S	O	B	E	G	C
H	O	L	D	F	A	S	H	I	O	N	E	D	O
A	E	Z	M	K	S	C	A	Y	G	Y	G	F	N
F	C	V	T	A	U	Z	R	P	A	O	C	L	T
S	L	X	G	B	F	R	M	A	U	D	O	T	E
H	J	W	V	X	V	A	I	C	M	Z	N	T	M
E	D	W	P	W	T	P	N	R	Z	P	V	E	P
Q	R	C	M	J	M	W	G	K	C	U	E	Z	O
A	F	F	O	R	D	A	B	L	E	N	N	D	R
B	T	N	T	Z	L	J	D	I	O	R	I	M	A
U	H	N	V	R	Y	G	F	Q	U	E	E	T	R
Y	O	R	O	N	X	Q	G	N	O	Y	N	G	Y
C	H	N	P	T	K	M	C	Q	W	J	T	V	P

2 Complete the sentences with the adjectives below.

chilly • expensive • inconvenient • spacious • uninviting • unpleasant • warm

1 The room looked very _____. It was cold and dark, and the furniture looked uncomfortable.
2 We wanted to buy some designer furniture for our new house, but it was too _____ and we couldn't afford it.
3 My apartment doesn't have central heating. It's pretty _____ in winter.
4 Don't stay in that hotel. It's very _____; everything is dirty and old.
5 I want to buy a large loft apartment. They're often very light and _____.
6 Our vacation home was 45 minutes from the beach. It was very _____.
7 The new heating system keeps the house _____ all winter.

3 Write four sentences about your home. Use adjectives for home and place.

I love my bedroom. It's light and spacious.

1 _____
2 _____
3 _____
4 _____

Focus on phrasal verbs

4 Complete the text. Use the correct form of the phrasal verbs below.

cater to • move in • put together • take off

THE MODERN MOVE

12 | AUG

Last month, I (1) _____ to a spacious, modern apartment. It took me a long time to (2) _____ all my new furniture. It was very frustrating!

This is an interesting part of town and it really (3) _____ young professionals like me. The apartments are affordable, and there are a few nice places to go to: stores, restaurants, coffee shops… This area isn't very popular right now, but they say that it next year it is really going to (4) _____.

Home Sweet Home   1

so … that / such … that

5 Circle the correct alternatives.

It's **so** / **such** cold here in the winter that we use a heater all the time.

1. This is **so** / **such** an expensive area of town that I can't afford to buy an apartment here.
2. The living room was **so** / **such** small that we couldn't fit all of our furniture in.
3. The house was in **so** / **such** a convenient location that we were surprised it was affordable.
4. The rented apartment was **so** / **such** charming that they decided to try to buy it.
5. The noise from the bars next to our hotel was **so** / **such** bad that we moved to a quieter area.
6. My bedroom is **so** / **such** a mess that I can't find anything.

6 Join the sentences with *so* or *such*.

There has been a rise in energy prices. A lot of people can't afford to use their heating.
There has been such a rise in energy prices that a lot of people can't afford to use their heating.

1. Urhahn and Koolhaas are creative artists. Each new design is a surprise.
   _____
2. It was a hot day. We spent all day at the pool.
   _____
3. We worked hard. We were exhausted by the evening.
   _____
4. It was a big and spacious house. All six children had their own bedrooms.
   _____
5. The vacation homes in New England are charming. We go there every year.
   _____
6. My office is warm. I wear a T-shirt to work every day.
   _____

Conjunctions of purpose

7 Complete the conjunctions of purpose with one word only.

They sold their house in _order_ to save money.

1. She looked on the internet _____ see the cost of houses in that area.
2. He contacted a real estate agent in _____ to help him find a new apartment.
3. We moved house _____ that we would have more space.
4. The builder moved a wall _____ order to make the room more spacious.
5. We bought a mobile home so _____ to get away on the weekends.
6. They attended a workshop so _____ they could learn how to build their own home.

8 Circle the correct alternatives.

We need to borrow more money **in order to** / **so that** buy the apartment we want.

1. They moved to Miami **that** / **so that** they could be closer to their children.
2. She talked to an interior designer **so as to** / **so that** make the right decisions about the furniture.
3. We rented an apartment for a week **so that** / **to** see what the area was like.
4. Why don't you ask someone who lives there **so that** / **in order to** you can find out more about the area?
5. We bought some new furniture **in order to** / **so that** make the room feel more cozy.
6. My grandparents sold their big house **so that** / **so as to** buy a smaller apartment.

Language reference page 65

Grammar

Present perfect simple

1 Complete the chart with the past participles of the verbs. Write *R* (regular) or *I* (irregular).

spend	*spent*	*I*
1 buy	_____	___
2 visit	_____	___
3 find	_____	___
4 take	_____	___
5 move	_____	___
6 finish	_____	___

2 Complete the sentences with the present perfect form of the verbs in parentheses.

I *'ve spent* _____ (**spend**) all day with a real estate agent.
1 The builders _____ (**finish**) all the work on our new apartment.
2 We _____ (**not buy**) any new furniture because it's too expensive.
3 Ramon _____ (**move out**) of his parents' house to live with some friends.
4 I _____ (**not visit**) my hometown for a long time.
5 Those new designs _____ (**take off**) all around the world.
6 She _____ (**not find**) a new apartment yet.

3 Circle the correct alternatives.

Lidia Hi, Ben! (1) **Have you finished / Did you finish** your art project yet?
Ben No, not yet. My bedroom is so cramped and it's such a mess! I (2) **didn't see / haven't seen** my art project for three days! I (3) **have watched / watched** a DVD last night.
Lidia What (4) **have you watched / did you watch**?
Ben I (5) **have watched / watched** *Avengers Assemble*.
Lidia What (6) **has it been / was it** like?
Ben It was awesome, but (7) **I've seen / I saw** it twice already.
Lidia Why (8) **have you watched / did you watch** it again?
Ben It's a great movie, and it (9) **was / has been** better than finishing my art project!

4 Complete the e-mail. Use the present perfect or the past simple form of the verbs in parentheses.

Hi Steffi!
How are you? I *haven't heard* _____ (**not hear**) from you in a while. What's happening with you?
We are spending the week in southern California, visiting some friends. They (1) _____ (**live**) here for a year now and we (2) _____ (**not see**) them since they (3) _____ (**move**).
California is amazing! I (4) _____ (**never go**) to the West Coast before.
On Saturday morning, I (5) _____ (**go**) for a walk along the beach with my friend Linda. It's beautiful and there are some fantastic restaurants.
On Sunday, we (6) _____ (**do**) some shopping but I (7) _____ (**not buy**) anything. That's the first time I (8) _____ (**go**) shopping and come back with some money!
What (9) _____ you _____ (**do**) on the weekend?
Hope to see you soon,
Ella

92

Home Sweet Home

Present perfect continuous

5 Complete the sentences. Use the present perfect continuous form of the verbs below.

> build • clean • learn • live • ~~study~~ • work

My grandma _has been studying_ English for the past year.

1 _____ you _____? The house looks so neat!
2 I _____ to drive since my birthday.
3 They _____ that new hotel for a long time.
4 He _____ on this project for two months.
5 How long _____ your parents _____ in a mobile home?

6 Rewrite the sentences with *for* or *since* and the present perfect continuous.

I started working as an interior designer ten years ago. I still work as an interior designer now.

I _'ve been working as an interior designer for_ ten years.

1 We moved to Beijing in 2010. We still live there now.
   We _____ 2010.
2 He started studying architecture five years ago. He's still studying now.
   He _____ five years.
3 They're looking for a new house. They started looking three months ago.
   They _____ three months.
4 I started putting together this desk at 9 a.m. I'm still putting it together.
   I _____ 9 a.m.
5 My best friend is working as a tour guide. She started working a year ago.
   My best friend _____ a year.

7 Circle the correct alternatives.

Journalist Gloria Meades has recently won the Young Architect of the Year Award. Gloria, how long (1) **have you been wanting** / **have you wanted** to be an architect?

Gloria A long time! I (2) **'ve been loving** / **'ve loved** architecture since my parents took me to a design exhibition when I was eight years old. I (3) **'ve designed** / **'ve been designing** since then.

Journalist What kinds of buildings do you design?

Gloria Over the past few years, I (4) **'ve specialized** / **'ve been specializing** in designing urban spaces.

Journalist What does that involve?

Gloria I (5) **'ve been working** / **'ve worked** with recycled materials and trying to make buildings more environmentally-friendly.

Journalist And what's the most recent project that you (6) **'ve completed** / **'ve been completing**?

Gloria Well, I (7) **'ve been working on** / **'ve worked on** a new university building recently. It's almost finished, and I (8) **'ve been helping** / **'ve helped** my manager with the design for a new shopping mall, too.

Journalist That's great, thanks Gloria. Good luck!

Language reference pages 64–65

2 The World of Work
Reading

A Flexible Life
HOME BLOG ABOUT

downshift (verb) change to a job or style of life where you may earn less but which puts less pressure on you and involves less stress

AUG 18 — **Downshifting: can you have it all?**
Melissa Wilson-Day

1 The need to change
Eighteen months ago, I was a marketing executive in a Boston law firm. I was hard-working and earned a good salary. I should have been happy, but I was exhausted and stressed all the time, working 12-hour days. A friend told me I should take up Pilates to help me relax, so I started going to classes. The classes were great, but I still felt my work–life balance could be better. I really wanted to leave my current stressful lifestyle behind. Could downshifting be the answer?

2 _____
I started daydreaming about becoming my own boss. I wrote a list of requirements for my new career: fewer hours, more time to spend with family and friends, a healthier, more relaxed lifestyle… Finally, I decided that working as a Pilates instructor might be the solution. I liked the idea of instructing energizing workouts and working with satisfied clients. I even thought about starting a blog to give people health and fitness advice.

3 _____
In order to follow my dream, I signed up for a Pilates certification program and observed classes at the Boston Movement Institute. After a year, I got my certification, quit my marketing job, and set up a website to attract potential clients to my new business. I booked a room in a local fitness center and waited for my new relaxed lifestyle to begin.

4 _____
But living the dream is much harder than I thought. It turns out that you can't have it all! I must have been crazy to think that I would be able to work fewer hours with this job. I'm now working 14–16-hour days because I have to meet the demands of my clients. In addition, I have to update my website, find new clients, and set up new classes. In retrospect, I know I could have thought over more carefully some aspects of my new life and business. For example, I should have set myself a more realistic budget. However, I am certain that I shouldn't have waited so long to make the change. Despite the financial insecurity and the longer hours, I am feeling more fulfilled.

Write your comment here
You shouldn't be too hard on yourself. This is a terrific opportunity! You may want to consider using your valuable marketing skills to improve your business. You could advertise the business on social networking sites, or offer discounts on daily deal websites.
Antonio, San Diego

---

1 Skim the blog. Read statements 1–3. According to the blog, which are true?
1 Changing jobs always makes people happier.
2 People can change the way they work, use their skills in a different way, and be happier.
3 Downshifting can have problems and doesn't always make people happier.
A 1 only.   B 2 only.   C 3 only.   D 2 and 3.   E None.

2 Skim the blog again. Match headings A–E with each paragraph 1–4. There is one extra heading.
A The dream ____
B The preparation ____
C The reality ____
D The need to change __1__
E The benefits ____

The World of Work 2

3 Read the blog again. Choose the correct answers.

1 According to the dictionary definition, "downshifting" can mean …
 A changing jobs, earning more money, and feeling more stressed.
 B changing jobs, earning less money, and feeling happier.
 C staying in the same job, earning less money, and feeling less stressed.
 D finding a new job, earning less money, and feeling more pressure.
 E changing jobs, earning more money, and feeling less pressure.

2 Melissa dreamed of …
 A earning a better salary.
 B spending more time doing Pilates.
 C having a more challenging job.
 D writing a blog about being a Pilates instructor.
 E enjoying a more flexible lifestyle.

3 Before she quit her old job, Melissa …
 A didn't really know what she wanted to do.
 B spoke to a lot of people about what she should do.
 C trained for her new profession.
 D wasn't certain if her dream was going to be fulfilled.
 E talked to her own Pilates instructor.

4 Melissa now works …
 A fewer hours than she did before.
 B about the same amount as she did before.
 C only on the weekends.
 D harder than she did as a marketing executive.
 E only when she feels like it.

5 Melissa feels she …
 A may not have made the right decision.
 B is entirely happy with her change of job.
 C will continue working like this for a long time.
 D is happier now than she was before.
 E made her decision very carefully.

6 Antonio gives Melissa advice about …
 A other ways to continue as a Pilates instructor.
 B using her experience to help her new business.
 C alternative marketing job possibilities.
 D using social networks to promote her blog.
 E the value of her marketing skills.

4 Find words 1–6 in the blog. Circle the correct definition.

1 firm *(n)* (line 2)
 A a company you own yourself
 B a strong company
 C a business company

2 clients *(pl n)* (line 18)
 A people who buy things in stores
 B people who receive a service from a professional person
 C customers in a restaurant

3 quit *(v)* (line 23)
 A close down a computer program
 B leave a job
 C move to a different place to live

4 budget *(n)* (line 36)
 A a plan to save money
 B a lot of money
 C a plan to spend the money that is available

5 fulfilled *(adj)* (line 38)
 A completely happy and satisfied
 B very unhappy and dissatisfied
 C completely happy, but a bit dissatisfied

6 advertise *(v)* (line 42)
 A promote
 B warn
 C show

5 Read the blog again. What is the main idea?

A You should never quit your job.
B Careers and a big salary are more important than being happy.
C There is no point in changing your job if you're stressed and unhappy.
D If you're unhappy, you can change things and improve your quality of life.
E You should give up a stressful job even if you don't know what to do.

Vocabulary

Adjectives: personal qualities

1 Complete the adjectives with the missing vowels. Then answer the questions.

Are you and your friends h _a_ rd-w _o_ rk _i_ ng students?
Yes, we are.

1 Who is the most s ___ c ___ ___ b l ___ person you know?
_____

2 Are you an ___ n ___ r g ___ t ___ c person?
_____

3 Who is the most r ___ l ___ ___ b l ___ person in your class?
_____

4 How f l ___ x ___ b l ___ are you when things change?
_____

5 Are your friends c ___ n s ___ d ___ r ___ t ___ if you have a problem?
_____

6 Do you think best friends should be d ___ p ___ n d ___ b l ___?
_____

7 Do you prefer people who are ___ ___ t g ___ ___ n g or shy?
_____

2 Complete the sentences with the adjectives below.

adaptable • energetic • hard-working • kind • ~~outgoing~~ • reliable • sociable

My best friend at college is really friendly, and she really enjoys other people's company. She's very _outgoing_.

1 You're always so busy, but you never seem to be tired. You're very _____.
2 Alex doesn't mind changing his plans, and he deals with new situations easily. He's a very _____ person.
3 I have my own company. I work twelve hours a day, and I often work on the weekend. I'm very _____.
4 My boss trusts me and leaves me to work independently because she knows I'm _____.
5 Nurses are often very _____ people. They want to look after other people.
6 I'm going to work as a tour guide this summer because I enjoy talking with people and I'm really _____.

Focus on phrasal verbs

3 Complete verbs 1–4 with prepositions A–D.

A up   B behind   C over   D for

1 leave _____   3 think _____
2 account _____   4 take _____

4 Complete the sentences with the correct form of the verbs in exercise 3.

1 We've _____ your business proposal and we would like to hear more about it.
2 How can we _____ the decreased sales this year?
3 I decided to _____ a job as an aerobics instructor when I left my old firm.
4 Oh no! I've _____ my laptop _____ in the office.

The World of Work 2

Negative prefixes

5 Complete the chart with the adjectives below.

employed • flexible • legal • logical • obedient • organized • ~~possible~~
practical • replaceable • resistible • successful • sufficient

un-	il-	im-	in-	ir-	dis-
		possible			

6 Complete the sentences with the negative form of the **bold** adjectives.

I think it's _illegal_ to work in this country without a proper work permit. (**legal**)

1 You aren't telling me the truth. Don't be _____. (**honest**)
2 Some kids at school can be _____, calling other people names. (**kind**)
3 Sam never thinks about other people and is so _____. (**considerate**)
4 My colleague Nathan doesn't like waiting for anything. He's so _____. (**patient**)
5 Do you think it's _____ to ask someone how much they earn? (**polite**)
6 Martha didn't talk to anyone at the party. Some people thought she was _____. (**friendly**)

7 Write true sentences about people you know. Use adjectives with negative prefixes.

1 _____
2 _____
3 _____
4 _____

Easily-confused words

8 Correct the sentences. Replace the **bold** verbs with the verbs below.

borrow • earn • lend • lost • missed • remember • ~~remind~~ • say • tell • win

Remember me to call in order to find out about the interview time.
Remind me to call in order to find out about the interview time.

1 How much do top executives **win** each year?
_____

2 I **lost** my job interview yesterday because the bus was late.
_____

3 Can you **borrow** me that book on interview tips?
_____

4 My boss has **missed** her glasses again. That's four times this week!
_____

5 Did you **tell** anything to your parents about your promotion?
_____

6 I've forgotten their names. Can you **remind** them?
_____

7 How much money did you **earn** in the competition?
_____

8 Can you **say** me when I can start the job?
_____

9 You can't **lend** my laptop just now. I'm using it.
_____

Language reference page 67

Grammar

Modal verbs

1 What do the modal verbs in the sentences express? Write *A* (ability), *P* (possibility), or *D* (deduction).

I **can** run a kilometer in under five minutes. _A_

1 Alicia **might** downshift and become a gardener. ____
2 Congratulations on passing the English test! You **must** be so happy. ____
3 He **could** be an interior designer if he wanted to, but he prefers making things. ____
4 Sandra **may** not take up the new position in her company. ____
5 That **can't** be Pete's sister over there – he said she was away traveling this month. ____
6 My company is looking for an employee who **can** speak Spanish. Do you know anyone? ____

2 Choose the correct answers to complete the sentences.

She can speak good Spanish, so she ____ apply for the job in Chile.
A must   B can't   (C might)   D couldn't   E has to

1 Teachers ____ be very good at communicating with people.
   A can't   B might   C may   D must   E must not
2 She ____ work as a pilot because she has problems with her sight.
   A can't   B must   C might   D can   E could
3 I think doctors ____ be hard-working, patient, and kind.
   A can't   B must not   C might   D may   E have to
4 He has worked in three different countries in the last year. He ____ be very adaptable.
   A can't   B must   C might   D could   E can
5 I ____ work in my dad's company when I leave school. I haven't decided.
   A must   B can't   C may   D must not   E have to
6 I ____ work on the weekend. I only work Monday to Friday.
   A don't have to   B must   C might   D have to   E could

3 Read the tips. Circle the correct alternatives

JOB INTERVIEW TIPS

- You **should** / **don't have to** be organized.
- Make sure you know the name of the person you (**1**) **have to** / **don't have to** meet when you arrive.
- You (**2**) **must** / **must not** be late. Allow plenty of time to travel to the interview.
- You (**3**) **should** / **shouldn't** dress smartly. You (**4**) **must not** / **don't have to** wear a suit, but you (**5**) **should** / **must not** look professional. However, you (**6**) **don't have to** / **shouldn't** wear too much make-up, perfume, or aftershave.
- You (**7**) **don't have to** / **must not** lie in an interview, or include false information on your résumé. Employers usually know if you are being dishonest.
- You (**8**) **should** / **must not** ask questions at the end of the interview.
- You (**9**) **don't have to** / **must not** have a long list of questions, but it's useful to prepare a few in advance.
- If you (**10**) **should** / **have to** give a presentation, practice it with a friend before the interview.

The World of Work 2

Modal perfects

4 Circle the correct alternatives.

Adriana So, how's the new job?
Mike It's good, but I know I (1) **can't have / must have** made a very good impression on my first day.
Adriana What happened?
Mike I (2) **should have / can't have** tried to remember everyone's names, but I just couldn't. I called my boss Helen all day. Her name's Hannah.
Adriana That isn't a problem, is it?
Mike I'm not sure. She (3) **must have / couldn't have** thought I was very unprofessional.
Adriana Well, she (4) **might not have / might have** noticed.
Mike She (5) **must have / can't have** realized. I suppose I (6) **could have / couldn't have** said something, but I was too embarrassed. Then at the end of the day my boss said "Goodbye, Matt". I don't know if she was joking …

5 Complete the dialogues with a modal perfect. Use the verbs in parentheses.

1 A I used to work as a circus performer.
   B That _____ an interesting experience. (**must / be**)
2 A Is Pepe hard-working, talented, and intelligent?
   B Absolutely! He _____ any career he wanted. (**could / choose**)
3 A It's a shame that you missed the job fair.
   B I know. I _____ about some good jobs. (**might / find out**)
4 A Was Marisa really good at languages at school?
   B Yes. She _____ a translator, not a lawyer. (**should / be**)
5 A I sent off my application form three weeks ago, but I haven't heard anything yet.
   B Why don't you call the company? They _____ your application. (**may / not receive**)

6 Rewrite the sentences without changing the meaning. Use appropriate modal verbs or modal perfects.

It wasn't a good idea for Annie to start her new job this week.
Annie _shouldn't have started her new job this week._

1 It isn't certain that he will study architecture.
   He _____.
2 I'm sure David's boss was delighted when he discovered David was such a dependable and hard-working employee.
   David's boss _____.
3 I'd advise you to study for a certification before you look for a job.
   You _____.
4 It is obligatory for all employers to provide a safe working environment for employees.
   All employers _____.
5 It isn't obligatory for her to send in the application until next week.
   She _____.
6 She had the chance to take up a new job in Cairo, but she decided not to take it.
   She _____.

Language reference pages 66–67

3 Sports Heroes

Reading

1 Physically and mentally, running marathons is a huge challenge. Many people train for months in order to take on the 42 kilometer run. So, why do it? We answer some of your questions.

"I'm overweight, unfit, and haven't done any exercise in years. Is it too late to start now?"

2 Keeping fit and losing weight are two key reasons why people start running marathons, and it's never too late for that! Just remember to take it easy at first. Andrea Starr was 52 when she started running again. "I used to be very petite and I had done a lot of running when I was young. When I retired, I decided to talk to my doctor about healthy ways to lose weight." Her doctor explained that running can have long-term health benefits for people of all ages: reduced risk of heart disease, diabetes, and joint problems in later life. The key is to warm up properly, start with slow, gentle runs, set demanding but achievable goals – and make sure you stretch afterward! Changing your diet will help you lose weight and run better, too. Eat healthy food like lean meat, fish, fruit, and vegetables, and have a small snack before you run. Andrea has now run three marathons and is training for her next one.

"How do I find enough time or energy to train?"

3 Taking time out for running may be easier than you think. Jerry Leavis has a very busy lifestyle, with a young family and a full-time job that involves a lot of travel. He used to do team sports, but hadn't had much time for exercise in recent years. However, running proved to be a convenient alternative. "I don't need any special equipment: just an open space and my sneakers!" Jerry now runs during his lunch hour and fits in regular runs when he's traveling. "I'm a very competitive person, so I recently signed up to run a half-marathon."

"42 kilometers is such a long distance! What's the point?"

4 Many people run marathons to raise money for charity. Selena Mason had already run several half-marathons, but when her best friend died of cancer two years ago, she decided to take on a bigger challenge in her memory. "Before she died, my friend had started to do a lot of charity work, so I wanted to find a way to support the charities she believed in." Selena has now run three full marathons, raising $3,500 for different cancer charities. "It is still about my friend, but it's also about proving to myself that I can tolerate the mental and physical challenges."

1 Skim the magazine article quickly. Choose the best title.

A A short history of the marathon
B Running is just for the young
C Advanced marathon running
D Pushing the limits
E Marathon running for body and soul

Sports Heroes

2 Read the article again. Choose the correct answers.

1. Many people start running because they want to …
   - A take it easy while they are losing weight.
   - B lose weight and keep fit.
   - C lose weight quickly.
   - D keep fit even though they are overweight.
   - E have a healthy diet and keep fit.

2. Andrea began running again …
   - A after she retired.
   - B after a friend of hers had died.
   - C in her twenties.
   - D because she wanted to get fit.
   - E because her doctor told her to.

3. Andrea …
   - A did not ask for any advice before she started running marathons.
   - B asked for advice before she started running marathons.
   - C had joint problems before she started running marathons.
   - D had to diet before she started running.
   - E is planning to run her first marathon next year.

4. Jerry decided to start running because …
   - A he was very busy and stressed.
   - B he had a lot of spare time for running.
   - C it was easy to fit into his busy lifestyle.
   - D he's a competitive person.
   - E he ran competitively when he was younger.

5. For some people, marathon running is a good way to …
   - A raise money for your friends.
   - B prove to yourself that you can raise money.
   - C avoid doing charity work.
   - D prove that you have friends.
   - E raise money for charities that are important to you.

3 Find expressions 1–6 in the article. Match them with definitions A–F.

1. losing weight (line 8) ___
2. take it easy (line 10) ___
3. warm up (line 18) ___
4. taking time out (line 27) ___
5. signed up (line 35) ___
6. raise money (line 38) ___

- A relax and avoid working too hard
- B committed yourself to a project or course of action
- C becoming less heavy
- D bring or collect money together
- E do gentle exercise to prepare for physical exercise
- F spending time away from your usual work or activity in order to rest

4 Answer the questions in your own words.

1. Why is running good for your health in general?
   _____
2. Why can running be a good sport to take up if you are busy?
   _____
3. Why do some people find running marathons a positive experience?
   _____
4. Why can running be good for overweight people?
   _____

5 According to the article, which statements are true?

- A A special diet is important when you are planning to run a marathon.
- B Inexperienced runners should start running gently before building up to marathons.
- C Anyone can run a marathon without training.
- D Running can reduce the risk of some diseases.
- E You can eat what you like if you do a lot of running.

Vocabulary

Adjectives: physical attributes

1 Read definitions 1–6. Choose the correct answers.

1 attractive; pretty
 A cute   B slim   C huge

2 thin in an attractive way
 A huge   B slender   C overweight

3 physically powerful
 A slim   B petite   C strong

4 very small
 A weak   B tiny   C huge

5 too heavy or fat
 A weak   B slender   C overweight

6 unattractive
 A ugly   B strong   C huge

2 Complete the sentences with the correct words in parentheses.

Australian Olympic Competitors, 2012 — Cate Campbell, Craig Mottram, Jenna O'Hea, Kynan Maley, Sally Pearson

1 Canoeist Kynan Maley is in his thirties but he's still very _____. (**weak / powerful**)
2 Athlete Sally Pearson is _____, but very fast. (**petite / huge**)
3 Swimmer Cate Campbell is very tall and _____. (**slim / overweight**)
4 Runner Craig Mottram is _____, which is unusual for a long distance runner. (**huge / tiny**)
5 Do you think Jenna O'Hea, the basketball player, is _____? (**good-looking / weak**)

3 Describe yourself or a member of your family. Use the words in exercises 1 and 2.

I am not good-looking or ugly, I am average! I am slim, ...

Focus on phrasal verbs

4 Complete the verbs 1–4 with prepositions A–D.

 A down   B off   C on   D up

1 bring _____   2 close _____   3 see _____   4 take _____

5 Complete the sentences. Use the correct form of the phrasal verbs in exercise 4.

1 The sports store in town _____. Now there isn't anywhere to buy sports equipment.
2 He _____ his opponents with some very skillful moves in last week's game.
3 I _____ my children to be polite and respectful.
4 The experienced chess player decided to _____ the junior champion in a charity event.

Sports Heroes 3

too / not … enough

6 Complete the sentences with *too* or *enough*.

We were *too* tired to finish the half marathon.

1 The wrestler wasn't powerful _____ to take on all four opponents.
2 I'm _____ lazy to work out at the gym every day.
3 They're _____ weak to lift those heavy weights.
4 He doesn't look tall _____ to be a good basketball player.
5 She isn't strong _____ to swim across the river.
6 Sebastian is _____ overweight. He should go on a diet.

7 Rewrite the sentences without changing the meaning. Use *too* or *not … enough* and the adjectives below.

> cheap • cold • early • fast • overweight • ~~short~~ • weak

I'd like to play in my college basketball team, but I'm not tall enough.
I'd like to play in my college basketball team, but I'm too short.

1 She was too slow to finish the race in first place.
_____

2 He isn't slim enough to run a marathon.
_____

3 We wanted to go to the beach, but it wasn't warm enough.
_____

4 I'll get tickets to the baseball game if they aren't too expensive.
_____

5 We weren't strong enough to beat the other team.
_____

6 We wanted to hear the talk on the Olympics, but we arrived too late.
_____

Noun suffixes (1)

8 Write the nouns from the verbs.

amuse *amusement*

1 imitate _____
2 prefer   _____
3 promote _____
4 endure   _____
5 organize _____
6 employ   _____

9 Complete the sentences with the nouns in exercise 8.

The cat caused a lot of *amusement* when it ran onto the field. Everyone was laughing.

1 It can be very difficult to find _____ as a professional sportsperson.
2 The team was very happy about its _____ to the top basketball league.
3 Running a marathon is a test of _____. It's very long.
4 You can watch whichever TV show you want. I have no _____.
5 I used to work for a huge _____ that sends disadvantaged kids to sports camps.
6 Everyone laughed at Simon's _____ of his boss. He sounded exactly like him.

Language reference page 69

Grammar

Past perfect

1 Complete the chart.

Infinitive	Simple past	Past participle
come	came	come
1 buy	_____	_____
2 forget	_____	_____
3 plan	_____	_____
4 read	_____	_____
5 sleep	_____	_____
6 visit	_____	_____

2 Complete the text. Use the correct past perfect form of the verbs in parentheses.

Dani _had moved_ (move) to the US to become a professional soccer player. His mother (1) _____ (bring) him up on her own, and she (2) _____ (work) very hard to support him and his soccer career. She (3) _____ (plan) to visit him in the US so she (4) _____ (save) the money for the airfare and she (5) _____ (buy) her ticket. It was the first time she (6) _____ (travel) on her own, and her first time on an airplane. She was very excited! However, when she got to the airport, she realized she (7) _____ (forget) her passport.

Past perfect and simple past

3 Circle the correct meanings.

The athlete had finished the race when he fell over.
- A The athlete fell over before he finished the race.
- (B) The athlete fell over after he finished the race.

1 Before I studied sports science, I hadn't thought about the importance of a good diet.
   - A I didn't think about the importance of a good diet before I studied sports science.
   - B I didn't think about the importance of a good diet after I studied sports science.

2 After her husband had moved abroad to work, she brought the children up on her own
   - A Her husband moved abroad to work. She then brought the children up on her own.
   - B Her husband moved abroad to work. She was already bringing the children up on her own.

3 When we arrived at the training ground, the rain had started.
   - A The rain started before we arrived.
   - B The rain started after we arrived.

4 The referee blew his whistle because he had seen a player with an injury.
   - A The referee saw a player with an injury and then blew his whistle.
   - B The referee blew his whistle and then he saw a player with an injury.

5 The game had started when the lights went out in the stadium.
   - A The lights went out in the stadium before the game started.
   - B The lights went out in the stadium after the game started.

6 After I had watched a few handball games, I decided to learn how to play.
   - A I decided to learn how to play handball before I saw a few games.
   - B I watched a few handball games. Then I decided how to learn how to play.

Sports Heroes 3

4 Circle the correct alternatives.
1 I **finished / had finished** the autobiography by the time we reached the airport.
2 We **had watched / watched** the game live on TV yesterday.
3 **Did you meet / Had you met** any coaches at the presentation last night?
4 They **weren't / hadn't been** on a plane until they traveled to the Olympic Games.
5 **Had you done / Did you do** any research on sports injuries during your course?
6 Annie **didn't study / hadn't studied** physiotherapy when she was at college.

5 Complete the sentences. Use the simple past and the past perfect in each sentence.

Before I _started_ (start) going to the gym, I _hadn't thought_ (not think) much about the importance of keeping fit!

1 I _____ (not be) very interested in any sort of exercise until I _____ (talk) to a fitness trainer.
2 After the doctor _____ (examine) me, he _____ (do) lots of different tests.
3 I _____ (have) high blood pressure and problems with my diet until I _____ (start) running
4 Before I _____ (see) a fitness coach, I _____ (not make) the connection between a healthy diet and a healthy lifestyle.

6 Join the sentences. Use a simple past verb and a past perfect verb.

The referee spoke to all the players. The game started.
By the time _the game started, the referee had spoken to all the players_.

1 We finished our workout. We left the gym.
   As soon as _____.
2 It stopped raining. Then we went to the beach to play volleyball.
   When _____.
3 They heard about a sport charity helping street children in Africa. Then they set up their own charity.
   After _____.
4 I visited the museum in the Yankees stadium. Then I watched a baseball game.
   I _____ before I _____.

7 Complete the text. Use the correct past perfect or the simple past form of the verbs in parentheses.

Henry Cejudo is very strong and at the age of 21 he _was_ (be) the youngest American to win an Olympic gold medal for wrestling. Henry (1) _____ (not have) an easy childhood. His parents (2) _____ (travel) to California from Mexico before he was born in the hope of a better life.
In 1991, Henry's mother Nelly (3) _____ (make) the difficult decision to bring her six children up on her own. Nelly (4) _____ (have to) work hard to support her family and they (5) _____ (move) around many times before the family finally settled in Phoenix, Arizona. The six Cejudo children (6) _____ (live) in poverty since they were born. They (7) _____ (sleep) on the floor and did not know when they might eat.
Henry (8) _____ (decide) from an early age that he would work hard at school to try and give himself a better future. After his brother Angel (9) _____ (introduce) him to wrestling, Henry (10) _____ (work) hard to prove himself to his father and to the rest of the world. He certainly succeeded.

Language reference page 68

4 A Career in Music

Reading

Trendsetters

Home | Young Entrepreneurs | About us

Hype Machine

Anthony Volodkin is someone who loves to follow the latest trends in music. Before he started his website, Hype Machine, he used to spend a lot of time reading music magazines, downloading music, listening to radio stations, and surfing music blogs to find out about cool new music. He also spent weekends
5 traveling to cities where he could see new bands perform. Volodkin thought that there must be an easier way to find out about the hottest new music. So in 2005 he started Hype Machine.

Hype Machine is a website where you can listen to your favorite music, read blogs about musicians and bands, and find new music. It displays the latest
10 posts from about 850 music blogs that Volodkin's employees select every week. Furthermore, it provides links so that users can purchase songs online, and buy tickets for upcoming shows. The site also has a popular "dashboard" feature which allows users to list their favorite tracks, blogs, songs, and other users who they like. Users can then share this information with their friends, by
15 linking their dashboard lists to their personal social network accounts.

Today, Hype Machine is one of the most popular music websites, with 1.2 million users who visit the site 13 million times a month. The website is free to use, but Volodkin makes money by taking a percentage from sales of songs and concert tickets, and through advertising.

Name: Anthony Volodkin
Location: New York City, US
Website: Hype Machine
Launched website: 2005
Employees: Five full-time; three part-time

scoreAscore

20 Jordan Passman used to work for the American Society of Composers, Authors, and Publishers. He knew it was difficult for composers to get music buyers to listen to their music, as there weren't many places where they could promote themselves. So, in 2008, he decided to develop a website that could set up deals between composers and music buyers for movies, commercials,
25 and other media productions.

Music buyers use Passman's website, scoreAscore, to post descriptions of the music that they need. The website has a database of 200 professional composers who write new music in response to these requests, or who upload music that they have already composed.

30 Composers whose music is accepted by the music buyers can earn a lot of money. On average, each piece of music on scoreAscore is sold for more than $1,000. Passman makes money by taking 40% of the composers' fees.

Name: Jordan Passman
Location: Los Angeles, US
Website: scoreAscore
Launched website: 2010; planning began 2008
Employees: None
2011 revenue: $300,000

1. Look at the photos. What do you think the men have in common? Skim the article and check your answer.

2. Find numbers 1–6 in the article. Match them with facts A–F.

1 850 _____ A the cost of an average transaction on scoreAscore
2 1.2 million _____ B the number of times that users visit Hype Machine each month
3 13 million _____ C the number of music blogs that Hype Machine uses
4 200 _____ D the number of people who use Hype Machine
5 $1,000 _____ E the number of professional composers who write music for scoreAscore
6 40 _____ F the percentage that Passman earns for sales of music

A Career in Music 4

3 Read statements 1–4. According to the article, are they true *(T)* or false *(F)*? Give evidence from the article.

Anthony Volodkin didn't know how to find out about new music. _F_
He used to read music magazines, download music, listen to radio stations, and read different music blogs.

1 Volodkin doesn't choose the music blogs to display on the website. ____
____

2 Hype Machine reviews music from other blogs. ____
____

3 Passman used to be a composer. ____
____

4 Passman doesn't employ anyone. ____
____

4 Read the article again. Choose the correct answers.

1 Volodkin started Hype Machine because he …
  A wanted to start a new band.
  B wanted to promote his band's cool new music.
  C wanted all the information about new music to be in one place.
  D enjoyed listening to cool music.
  E had seen some new bands, but didn't know anything about them.

2 Hype Machine currently has …
  A few full-time members of staff.
  B five part-time members of staff.
  C no other members of staff apart from Volodkin.
  D dozens of members of staff.
  E eight members of staff who don't all work full-time.

3 Hype Machine …
  A has its own social network.
  B allows users to link with their own social network page.
  C is looking into developing a social network.
  D sells a lot of music through social networks.
  E uses social networks to tell users what to buy.

4 In 2008, Passman started a website because …
  A some composers asked him to start it.
  B a lot of composers needed work.
  C he wanted to help composers promote themselves.
  D he wanted to be a composer and promote himself.
  E music buyers wanted him to find new composers.

5 scoreAscore works by …
  A music buyers posting their requirements on it.
  B Passman contacting media production companies himself.
  C composers telling music buyers what music they have written.
  D Passman telling composers what music to write.
  E people posting popular music on the website.

6 Passman earns money by …
  A sharing fees equally with the composers.
  B taking more money than the composers.
  C charging people $1,000 to use his website.
  D taking part of the composers' fees.
  E only selling existing music.

5 Find sentences 1–5 in the article. Who or what do the pronouns in **bold** refer to?

1 … **he** used to spend a lot of time reading music magazines … ____
2 **It** displays the latest posts … ____
3 … and other users who **they** like. ____
4 … in 2008, **he** decided to develop a website … ____
5 … upload music that **they** have already composed. ____

6 Look at the cartoon. Choose the best caption.

A Mom! I don't understand Grandpa's computer!
B Mom! Where are my headphones?
C Mom! How do you work Grandpa's laptop?
D Mom! How do you work Grandpa's MP3 player?
E Mom! This MP3 player is too loud!

Vocabulary

Verbs: music

1 Choose the correct answers to complete the sentences.

1 Here's the studio where we ___ a new album.
   A recorded   B released

2 Radiohead ___ *The King of Limbs* album online.
   A released   B composed

3 Rihanna is on tour this month because she is ___ her new album.
   A downloading   B promoting

4 Tom Jobim wrote a lot of music. He ___ the song *The Girl from Ipanema*.
   A promoted   B composed

5 Have you ___ Roberto Fonseca's new album yet?
   A composed   B downloaded

6 Do famous bands ___ and play a lot together before they give a concert?
   A record   B practice

7 Maroon 5 often ___ before a big tour by doing a few small concerts.
   A rehearse   B release

8 Adele ___ in Seattle during her US tour.
   A performed   B downloaded

2 Complete the texts with the words below. Then write the names of the singer and the group.

> performed • promote • recorded • released

Her real name is Onika Tanya Maraj. She (**1**) _____ her debut album, *Pink Friday*, in 2010 and she invented a character called Roman Zolanski to help (**2**) _____ it. She has (**3**) _____ songs with Rihanna and Will.i.am. She has also (**4**) _____ on tour with Britney Spears.

Who is she? _____

> composed • download • practiced • rehearse

They met on the UK TV show *The X Factor* where they auditioned as individuals, but the judges decided to form a group, so the boys had to (**5**) _____ together. One of the band members, Niall loved playing the guitar when he was young and he (**6**) _____ every day. He now enjoys writing music for the band, although he doesn't play guitar for them. Kelly Clarkson (**7**) _____ one of the songs on their first album, *Up All Night*. They did their first US tour in 2012. You can (**8**) _____ all of their songs online.

Who are they? _____

Focus on phrasal verbs

3 Match sentences 1–4 with sentences A–D.

1 The singer couldn't stop shaking after she came off the stage. ___
2 One of the singers had an amazing voice. ___
3 The band U2 do a lot of work for charity. ___
4 The audience was very noisy at the start of the concert. ___

A Everyone settled down though after a few minutes.
B That's why their fans look up to them.
C She found it very hard to wind down after the audition.
D He stood out from all the other singers in the competition.

Exercise 2   1 Nicki Minaj   2 One Direction

108

A Career in Music 4

Gerunds and infinitives (1)

4 Complete the sentences with the gerund or infinitive form of the verbs in parentheses.

1. My new girlfriend can't stand _____ (**listen**) to hip-hop music. I love it.
2. Our band needs _____ (**practice**) at least three hours a day before our next gig.
3. I want _____ (**go**) to the Jay-Z concert next weekend.
4. I would like _____ (**lend**) my brother's keyboard to my best friend, but he won't let me.
5. Do you enjoy _____ (**go**) to pop concerts?

5 Write sentences and questions. Use a gerund or *to* + infinitive.

1. He / loves / listen to classical music
   _____
2. We can't stand / go / to outdoor concerts / when it's raining
   _____
3. you / prefer / perform / or / attend / concerts ?
   _____
4. What / you / want / do / on the weekend ?
   _____
5. He doesn't mind / watch / *Pop Idol* / on TV
   _____
6. We hope / release / our latest song online / next month
   _____

6 Complete the sentences with your own ideas. Use a gerund or an infinitive in each sentence.

1. After school, I enjoy _____
   _____.
2. On the weekends, I like _____
   _____.
3. In the summer, I can't stand _____
   _____.
4. When I leave school, I want _____
   _____.

Noun suffixes (2)

7 Complete the definitions with the suffixes below.

| -ist • -or • -ian • -r • -ist • -ist • -er |

This is a painting by a modern art *ist* called Beatriz Milhazes. I love the colors.

1. The reception_____ at the hotel was very helpful.
2. There was a magic_____ at the children's party. They loved all his tricks.
3. The movie direct_____ had to tell the actors what to do in each scene.
4. I love doing experiments and finding out about chemical reactions. I'm going to be a scient_____.
5. My favorite write_____ is Paul Auster. He writes great novels.
6. Alicia Keys is great in concert. She is a fantastic sing_____.

Language reference page 71

Grammar

Relative clauses (1)

1 Read the text. Circle the correct alternatives.

Chris Martin is a talented singer and musician (**who**) / where has become one of the most famous names in music. He started a band in 1996 (**1**) which / when was called Pectoralz with his friend Jonny Buckland (**2**) who / which is a guitarist. They often played gigs in London, (**3**) where / that they were at college. Guy Berryman and Will Champion joined in 1998, and that was the year (**4**) when / which the band changed its name to Coldplay.

Over the last fifteen years, Coldplay has become one of the world's biggest bands. The young men (**5**) who / where met at college can't have imagined that they would ever be so famous.

There are a lot of companies worldwide (**6**) who / where want to use Coldplay's music to promote their products, but Coldplay have refused. Instead, the band donates money to charities because they want to help people (**7**) who / when are suffering around the globe. Coldplay is a band (**8**) that / where has a social conscience and (**9**) whose / which music continues to win big music prizes and awards.

2 Look at your answers in exercise 1. Write the noun or noun phrase that each relative pronoun refers to.

who – Chris Martin

1 _____ 4 _____ 7 _____
2 _____ 5 _____ 8 _____
3 _____ 6 _____ 9 _____

3 Complete the dialogues with a suitable relative pronoun. More than one answer may be possible.

1 A What's your favorite Beyoncé song?
  B There's a song called *Countdown* _____ is one of my favorites.

2 A Is New York the city _____ Lady Gaga was born?
  B I think so.

3 A Who sang the soundtrack in that movie?
  B I'm not sure, but I know the director _____ made it didn't speak English.

4 A What's the best time of year to go to outdoor concerts?
  B Well, July and August are the months _____ the weather is best.

5 A Who's Ryan Cabrera?
  B He's a singer _____ father is Colombian and _____ mother is American.

4 Match the beginnings of sentences 1–5 with the ends of sentences A–E and join them with a relative pronoun.

My sister has a college friend

1 A Fender Stratocaster is a guitar
2 2012 was the year
3 Adele is the singer
4 This is the house in Buenos Aires
5 Luciana Gimenez is the Brazilian host of *Super Pop*

A is very popular with professional musicians.
B Bruno Mars toured Brazil for the first time.
C album *21* won a Grammy Award in 2012.
D now lives in New York.
E the singer and songwriter, Carlos Gardel, grew up.
F plays the drums like Tre Cool in Green Day.

My sister has a college friend who plays the drums like Tre Cool in Green Day.

1 _____
2 _____
3 _____
4 _____
5 _____

A Career in Music 4

5 Read the sentences. Cross out any relative pronouns that you can omit.

Listen! Is this the singer ~~who~~ you like?

1 I really like the band whose singer performed at our prom.
2 This is the website that they recommended for downloading music apps.
3 This is the place where I met a famous singer.
4 I don't know the man who used to live in that house.
5 Is that the shop where David bought his electronic keyboard?
6 I really like the album which Matt lent me.

6 Circle the correct alternatives.
1 Is Emeli Sandé the singer **whose** / who's music you like?
2 My parents met someone on vacation who's / **whose** son knew Jay-Z!
3 **Who's** / Whose the best hip-hop artist at the moment, in your opinion?
4 I don't know **who's** / whose singing I prefer, Adele or Taylor Swift?
5 Do you know **who's** / whose singing at the Grammy awards?
6 Is that the boy **who's** / whose performing on *American Idol* next week?

7 Join the sentences with an appropriate relative pronoun.

A man works for a record company. He signed the new band immediately.
A man who works for a record company signed the new band immediately.

1 Madonna is a singer. Her twelfth studio album was called *MDNA*.
   _____

2 Consumers download albums from the internet. They contribute to the lack of CD sales in stores.
   _____

3 Jordan likes reading music blogs. They tell him about cool new music.
   _____

4 Letizia is a musician. She performs every weekend in local clubs.
   _____

5 Jazz is a popular kind of music. It originated in the US.
   _____

6 I'll show you my studio. I practice and rehearse there every day.
   _____

8 Complete the sentences with a relative pronoun and a phrase below.

> also runs a restaurant there • Emeli Sandé is playing • has a calendar for all the latest gigs • ~~like to go to listen to live music~~ • you can hear new pop and folk artists •

In San Francisco, I have a favorite place *where I like to go to listen to live music*.
1 It's a club called The Café du Nord _____
2 The owner of the club is a really nice man _____
3 There's a page on the website _____
4 I want to go there _____

5 Different Worlds

Reading

Growing up around the world

A rite of passage is an event that marks a new phase in a person's life. Different cultures have different ways of marking these phases. One important rite of passage for many cultures is the transition from childhood to adulthood. This is when a young person may try out the lifestyle they are about to enter, or experience a period of hardship to prepare them for adulthood.

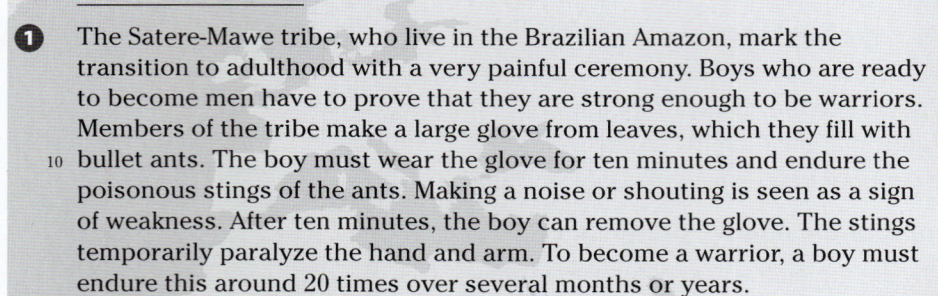

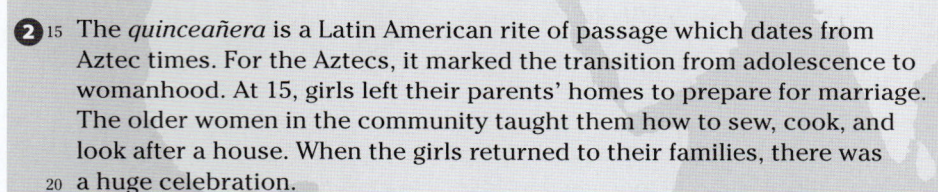

1 The Satere-Mawe tribe, who live in the Brazilian Amazon, mark the transition to adulthood with a very painful ceremony. Boys who are ready to become men have to prove that they are strong enough to be warriors. Members of the tribe make a large glove from leaves, which they fill with bullet ants. The boy must wear the glove for ten minutes and endure the poisonous stings of the ants. Making a noise or shouting is seen as a sign of weakness. After ten minutes, the boy can remove the glove. The stings temporarily paralyze the hand and arm. To become a warrior, a boy must endure this around 20 times over several months or years.

2 The *quinceañera* is a Latin American rite of passage which dates from Aztec times. For the Aztecs, it marked the transition from adolescence to womanhood. At 15, girls left their parents' homes to prepare for marriage. The older women in the community taught them how to sew, cook, and look after a house. When the girls returned to their families, there was a huge celebration.

Many countries still observe this tradition, but the *quinceañera* is now usually a big party where the girl wears an elaborate dress, which often looks like a wedding gown. In some celebrations, the girl's father dances the first dance, which is a waltz, with his daughter.

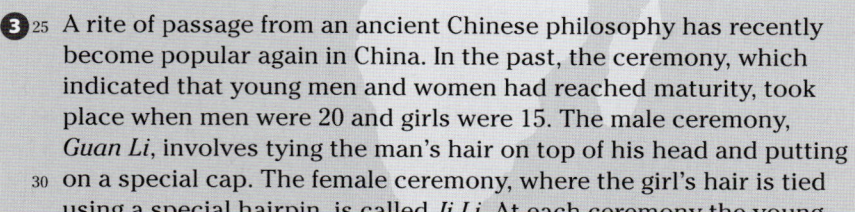

3 A rite of passage from an ancient Chinese philosophy has recently become popular again in China. In the past, the ceremony, which indicated that young men and women had reached maturity, took place when men were 20 and girls were 15. The male ceremony, *Guan Li*, involves tying the man's hair on top of his head and putting on a special cap. The female ceremony, where the girl's hair is tied using a special hairpin, is called *Ji Li*. At each ceremony the young people also receive their "style name," or adult name, whose use is a sign of respect. Nowadays, both men and women take part in this ceremony when they are 18.

1 Look at the photos. Where do you think the people are from? Skim the article and check.

2 Read the article again. Match headings A–D with paragraphs 1–3. There is one extra heading.

A Community life   B Dance the night away   C Ancient beliefs   D Warrior training

Different Worlds 5

3 Find nouns 1–6 in the article. Match them with definitions A–F.

1 transition ____
2 warrior ____
3 stings ____
4 adulthood ____
5 sew ____
6 tying ____

A a person who fights in a battle or war
B the process or period of changing from one state or condition to another
C the state of being an adult
D to use a needle and thread to make stitches in cloth
E joining together a piece of string, rope, etc. with a knot
F injuries caused when an insect, plant etc. makes a small hole in your skin

4 Read the article again. Choose the correct answers.

1 Satere-Mawe boys can't make a noise while wearing the glove because it …
  A scares the ants.
  B may show other members of the tribe that they are weak.
  C makes the ants weak.
  D encourages the ant to stop stinging.
  E makes the glove weak and it falls off.

2 After taking off the glove, the boys …
  A lose all the feeling in their hands.
  B can't move their hands or arms again.
  C have difficulty moving their hands for ten minutes.
  D can't move their hand or arm for some time.
  E can't move at all for 20 minutes.

3 When Aztec girls left their families, they …
  A learned new skills.
  B got married.
  C taught other women to cook.
  D had a big celebration.
  E never saw their parents again.

4 Nowadays the *quinceañera* is …
  A not celebrated anywhere.
  B still celebrated in exactly the same way.
  C a dance for a girl and her father.
  D a wedding celebration.
  E still celebrated, but in a more modern way.

5 The *Guan Li* and *Ji Li* ceremonies have their origins in …
  A a modern religious practice.
  B a modern system of beliefs.
  C a very old system of beliefs.
  D a new idea for Chinese communities.
  E an old idea about how to style hair.

6 The *Guan Li* and *Ji Li* ceremonies …
  A are exactly the same.
  B aren't similar.
  C are when the participants change their names.
  D are when the participants cut their hair.
  E aren't respectful to the participants.

5 Answer the questions in your own words.

1 Why are bullet ants used as part of the Satere-Mawe glove tradition?
_____

2 What was the significance of the *quinceañera* celebration in Aztec times?
_____

3 What do girls often wear in modern *quinceañera* celebrations? Why?
_____

4 What is the significance of the *Guan Li* and *Ji Li* ceremonies?
_____

5 Why do the *Guan Li* and *Ji Li* ceremonies include giving a "style name"?
_____

6 Which pair of statements are both correct, according to the article?

1 A Rites of passage can involve wearing special items of clothing.
  B Rites of passage can involve pain and hardship.

2 A Some cultures have adapted ancient traditions for modern society.
  B Some cultures have invented new rites of passage for modern society.

Vocabulary

Verbs: lifestyle choices

1 Choose the correct answers to complete the sentences.

1 Some teenagers find it hard to ____ their parents' advice.
  A follow   B guide   C allow   D experience
2 Do people at your school ____ a strict dress code?
  A worship   B abstain   C explore   D observe
3 Do the Amish ____ together or alone?
  A allow   B guide   C worship   D observe
4 Have you ever tried to ____ from eating chocolate?
  A abstain   B observe   C follow   D experience
5 I'd like to ____ the roots of my culture and language in more detail.
  A allow   B guide   C worship   D explore
6 Do you think life is easier if you have a religion to ____ you?
  A follow   B observe   C guide   D experience
7 Do you think our parents will ____ us to go traveling on our own this summer?
  A worship   B allow   C abstain   D explore

2 Complete the text with the words below.

abstain • allow • experienced • guide • worship

NEWS
○ home   ○ sport   ○ entertainment   ○ animals   ○ message board

More than 30 years ago, an American linguist, Daniel Everett, went to the Brazilian Amazon to explore the life and culture of the Piraha tribe. The Piraha live on the Maici River in the Amazon and they don't often (1) _____ people from outside into their environment. Everett lived with the tribe for a long time, and he was surprised by what he (2) _____ there.

For example, he discovered that Piraha people often (3) _____ from food even when food is available. They have no words for colors or numbers, and no written language. And they do not (4) _____ a god or use religion to (5) _____ them through life.

Focus on phrasal verbs

3 Circle the correct meaning of the bold phrasal verbs.

1 Can you **bring up** the subject of teen lifestyles during the debate tomorrow?
  A raise children   B raise the topic of
2 The archaeologists **came across** some interesting documents while they were working.
  A found something by chance   B made a particular impression
3 Shall we **try out** that new exercise class tonight?
  A test something   B put on clothes to see if they fit
4 We looked at driving from Boston to San Diego. The length of the drive **put us off**.
  A delayed doing something   B caused us to lose interest or enthusiasm

4 Complete the sentences. Use the correct form of the phrasal verbs in exercise 3.

1 Shall we _____ that new restaurant for lunch today?
2 They _____ some difficult questions during the interview.
3 The price of flights _____ them _____ traveling to Australia.
4 Did you _____ my glasses when you were cleaning the living room?

Different Worlds 5

Gerunds and infinitives (2)

5 Circle the correct alternatives.

1 **To spend / Spending** time in a different culture can teach you a lot.
2 I want **to go / going** traveling on my own after college.
3 I've decided **to abstain / abstaining** from candy for a whole week.
4 Do we need **to share / sharing** our ideas for the research project with the others?
5 **To watch / Watching** that documentary really made me think about different ways of life.
6 After **to discuss / discussing** the Amish way of life, the students decide to explore the culture a bit more.

6 Complete the text with the gerund or infinitive form of the verbs in parentheses.

Australia | ABOUT Facts about Australia | EXPLORE Things to see and do | PLAN Plan your trip

Homepage > About > Australia's Culture

The indigenous people of Australia, the Aborigines, are proud _to have_ (**have**) a traditional rite of passage called "walkabout". (1) _____ (**walk**) alone in the outback for up to six months during adolescence was the key part of this tradition for male adolescents.

Before (2) _____ (**set out**) on their journey, the boys learned about their ancestors. Their aim was (3) _____ (**follow**) the paths of their ancestors in the outback. (4) _____ (**survive**), they ate tomatoes, nuts, seeds, and berries. After (5) _____ (**return**) home safely, there was a big celebration. Nowadays, many Aborigines still choose (6) _____ (**have**) a ceremony to celebrate the transition to adulthood. It is common for young Aborigines (7) _____ (**paint**) their bodies in the ceremony, and everyone enjoys (8) _____ (**sing**) and (9) _____ (**play**) traditional instruments.

Prefixes

7 Complete the table with the words below.

act • conformist • consider • crowding • disciplined • heard • make • national • react • smoking • sufficient • understanding

re-	mis-	over-	self-	non-	inter-
consider					

8 Complete the sentences with the correct words in exercise 7.

1 We'll have to _____ our travel options. All of the flights are fully booked.
2 There's a lot of _____ in cities today and more and more people are living in slums.
3 I prefer to sit in the _____ part of a restaurant.
4 There was obviously a _____ because they were waiting in different places.
5 All _____ flights leave from Terminal 2.
6 The Amish are a very _____ community and can provide what they need themselves.

Language reference page 73

Grammar

Relative clauses (2)

1 Read the text. Circle the correct alternatives.

Losing a world

Boa Sr, (**1**) **who / when** died in 2010, was the last living speaker of an ancient tribal language. She lived in the Andaman Islands in the Indian Ocean (**2**) **which / where** one of the world's oldest cultures had existed for 65,000 years. Boa Sr was the last person (**3**) **where / who** was fluent in the language of Bo. The loss of the language, (**4**) **which / whose** also means the loss of a whole community, is a serious issue for linguists and anthropologists.

Bo was one of the ten Great Andamanese languages, (**5**) **which / when** date back to pre-Neolithic times. However, since the mid-nineteenth century, (**6**) **who / when** European settlers colonized the islands, the tribal languages of Andaman have been in decline.

Another Andaman tribe, the Onge, (**7**) **who / whose** culture and history is also in danger, has fewer than 100 members left. Nowadays, new roads, (**8**) **which / where** join several of the islands, are attracting more settlers, but there are still some tribes in remote areas of the islands (**9**) **whose / who** remain independent of outside influences.

2 What kind of relative clause do these rules refer to? Write *D* (defining), *ND* (non-defining), or *B* (both).

They give essential information. _D_

1 They give extra information. ____
2 We can omit *which*, *who*, or *that* if it is not the subject of the clause. ____
3 We can use *that* instead of *which* or *who*. ____
4 We cannot omit *whose*. ____
5 We use commas to separate them from the rest of the sentence. ____
6 We never omit the relative pronoun. ____

3 Look at the relative clauses in exercise 1. Write *D* (defining) or *ND* (non-defining).

1 ____   4 ____   7 ____
2 ____   5 ____   8 ____
3 ____   6 ____   9 ____

4 Add commas to the sentences where necessary. Can you omit any relative pronouns?

The researcher, who is researching lost tribes in the Amazon, discovered a new tribe recently.

1 In some cultures, a special ceremony takes place when a boy reaches the age of thirteen.
2 Martin is the teacher who we met at the conference.
3 This is the website where there is a lot of information about different cultures.
4 The village that I go to on vacation with my family is very different from my own town.
5 My best friend who loves playing computer games never watches TV!
6 Daniel Everett is the linguist who spent a lot of time with the Piraha tribe.
7 Living abroad which a lot of young people choose to do is a good way to learn about other cultures.

Different Worlds 5

5 Correct the underlined part of each sentence. More than one answer may be possible.

These are some photos <u>that I took them</u> on vacation. *These are some photos that I took on vacation.*

1 This is the tour guide <u>who we met him</u> on the first morning.
   _____

2 I took this photo on the day <u>which we went</u> to see the volcano.
   _____

3 This is the place <u>who we ate</u> in the local market.
   _____

4 That's me in a poncho and hat <u>that I bought them</u> in the market.
   _____

5 This is the *casa particular* <u>that we stayed</u>.
   _____

6 These are the other people in our group <u>whose their names</u> I can't remember.
   _____

6 Circle the correct alternatives. If you can omit the relative pronoun, circle *[0]*. More than one answer may be possible.

That's the girl (who) / (that) / [0] is very self-sufficient and independent.

1 We went to a National Park **where / when / which** there were brown bears.
2 Scientists **who / whose / that** work in the South Pole are researching global warming.
3 Bo is another language **which / that / [0]** has died out recently.
4 The Amish are a people **who / that / [0]** don't use modern technology.
5 This is the hall **when / which / where** the local Quaker community meet every week.
6 Roald Amundsen was the first explorer **who / that / [0]** reached the South Pole.
7 Do you have a science book **which / that / [0]** I could borrow?
8 Piraha is a language **who / that / [0]** is usually spoken, not written.

7 Complete the text with appropriate relative pronouns. More than one answer may be possible.

On the island of Borneo _where_ the Ngaju Dayak people live, there is an important rite of passage for adolescent boys. The boys, (1) _____ carry only simple weapons, must go into the jungle alone to catch a wild boar or a monkey. These are animals (2) _____ the Ngaju Dayak people enjoy eating.

In the jungle, the boys must face difficult challenges: dangerous snakes (3) _____ bite is so poisonous that it can kill you within an hour, crocodiles (4) _____ live in the rivers, and neighboring tribes (5) _____ may attack if you walk into their territory.

When the boys return home with an animal (6) _____ they have killed, they go to a house in the village (7) _____ another member of the tribe gives them a tattoo to show they have completed their rite of passage. The boys, (8) _____ ancestors began this sacred tradition, will get more tattoos as they get older.

Language reference page 72

6 TV Trends

Reading

The allure of the infomercial

Infomercials are a familiar feature on late-night TV in the US. These feature-length advertisements, with their intriguing special offers and entertaining product demonstrations, encourage viewers to buy all kinds of products they never knew they needed. Fitness equipment, skin-care products, and time-saving household gadgets are often sold on infomercials, and viewers are encouraged to buy immediately via e-mail or phone. The infomercial phenomenon began in the US about 20 years ago, and it's an industry which is still growing.

BUT WAIT THERE'S MORE!

- 2006 $90 billion
- 2009 $91 billion
- 2011 $150 billion

Since 2006, late-night TV shopping has grown by 40%. More than $150 billion dollars of consumer products are sold in the US through infomercials each year.

How do infomercials work?

- An everyday problem is presented.
- An intriguing solution to the problem is demonstrated.
- The unbelievably cheap price is revealed, as well as a time limit to motivate customers to buy sooner.

Why do infomercials work?

Most infomercials are usually five to six minutes long and they are designed to increase the levels of dopamine in the brain. Dopamine is a chemical which is associated with addictive behavior. It motivates us to look for solutions to problems and makes us feel good when we achieve our goals.

The brain chemistry behind infomercials

- A problem is presented. The brain tries to think of a solution.
- Dopamine levels in the brain rise as a solution to the problem is demonstrated, increasing our impulse to buy.
- Viewers are told to "Buy now!"
- Dopamine levels fall after five to six minutes.

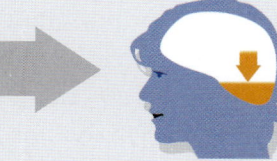

Who buys from infomercials?

70% Seven out of ten Americans have ordered a product from an infomercial at least once.

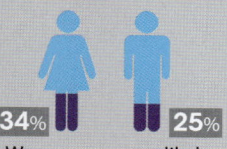

34% / **25%** Women are more likely to buy products from infomercials than men.

How successful are infomercials?

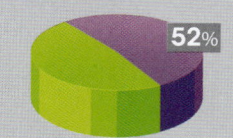

52% of customers are satisfied with their purchases.

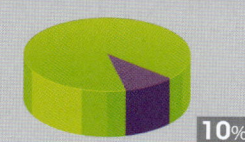

10% Only 10% of customers say they would buy a product from an infomercial again.

TV Trends 6

1 Skim the infographic. What is an infomercial?

A a short TV commercial
B a feature-length TV show
C a long TV commercial

2 Why do you think people buy from infomercials? Infer from the infographic.

A The products are better than in a store.
B They only have a limited time to buy.
C The infomercials are entertaining.
D The claims of the infomercials are convincing.
E They want to keep fit and have clean floors.

3 Read the infographic again. Choose the correct answers.

1 According to the infographic, the infomercial industry …
   A has declined over the last 20 years.
   B began about ten years ago.
   C gives presentations to sales people.
   D has grown over the last 20 years.
   E employs people to work late at night.

2 People spent $1 billion more on purchases from infomercials …
   A in 2009 compared with 2006.
   B in 2006 compared with 2009.
   C in 2011 compared with 2006.
   D in 2011 compared with 2009.
   E each year from 2006 to 2011.

3 Infomercials make you think that you …
   A must buy everything you see.
   B have a lot of problems at home.
   C can't buy the same products in a local store.
   D need a specific product for a specific problem.
   E want to clean you floors.

4 Dopamine is produced …
   A when we want to purchase something new.
   B when the brain tries to find a solution to a problem.
   C after watching five minutes of infomercials.
   D when we feel good about something.
   E after we watch an infomercial for five minutes.

5 In terms of purchases, … from infomercials.
   A women buy fewer things than men
   B men and women buy the same number of products
   C 9% more men make purchases than women
   D men buy fewer things than women
   E 34% of men make a purchase

6 Around 90% of people who buy something from an infomercial …
   A are happy with their purchases.
   B want to buy more products.
   C are not happy with their purchases.
   D return their products because they don't like them.
   E don't want to make another purchase.

4 Find words 1–6 in the text. Match them with definitions A–F.

1 demonstration ____
2 phenomenon ____
3 intriguing ____
4 motivate ____
5 addictive ____
6 impulse ____

A an event in nature or society, especially one that is not fully understood
B a strong and sudden wish to do something
C give someone a reason to want to do something
D showing or explaining how something works
E people need or want to do something as often as possible because they enjoy it
F very interesting because of being unusual

Vocabulary

Television

1 Choose the correct answers to complete the sentences.

1 Will Schuester is one of the main ____ in *Glee*.
 A viewers B characters C episodes

2 Some reality TV characters are ____ in a negative way.
 A filmed B cast C portrayed

3 It took three years to ____ each *Star Wars* movie.
 A film B broadcast C portray

4 Teri Hatcher was in the ____ of *Desperate Housewives*. She played Susan Mayer.
 A character B episode C cast

5 In season 8 of *American Idol*, ____ sent 178 million texts to vote for their favorite act.
 A viewers B characters C scenes

6 Matt Groening, who created *The Simpsons*, was also one of the ____ of *Futurama*.
 A viewers B producers C characters

7 The ninth ____ of the reality TV show *Top Chef* was filmed in Texas.
 A scene B viewer C season

8 All of the ____ in the movie *The Hunger Games* were filmed in North Carolina.
 A casts B scenes C seasons

9 The last episode of *House* was ____ in May, 2012. Hugh Laurie played the main character.
 A broadcast B filmed C cast

2 Complete the text with the words below.

> broadcast • cast • character • episode • filmed • portrays • producer • scenes • viewers

The sitcom, or situation comedy, is a TV show with a lot of jokes and entertaining dialogue. Sitcoms were originally **(1)** _____ on the radio, but most are now shown on TV.

A recent popular American TV sitcom is *New Girl*. The first **(2)** _____ was watched by 10.28 million **(3)** _____ when it was shown on Fox TV in September 2011. The **(4)** _____ includes actors Zooey Deschanel, Jake Johnson, and Max Greenfield. Zooey Deschanel worked closely with the show's **(5)** _____, Elizabeth Merriwether, to develop the **(6)** _____ of Jess Day, an elementary school teacher who has just broken up with her boyfriend. Deschanel **(7)** _____ Jess as an amusing, likeable young woman. A lot of the **(8)** _____ in the show are **(9)** _____ in Los Angeles.

Focus on phrasal verbs

3 Complete verbs 1–4 with *off*, *out*, or *up*.

1 fall _____   3 show _____
2 keep _____   4 make _____

4 Complete the comments. Use the correct form of the phrasal verbs in exercise 3.

1 Joey was telling everyone about his award nomination again. I hate it when he _____.
2 Francine said she saw Blake Lively downtown on the weekend. Do you think she _____ it _____?
3 I _____ with my boyfriend two days ago. We're still not talking to each other.
4 I was away last week. How can I _____ with what happened in my favorite TV show?

TV Trends 6

-ed and -ing adjectives

5 Replace the underlined phrases with the correct form of *be* and an adjective. Use the words in parentheses with *-ed* or *-ing*.

The storyline in that new TV sitcom isn't very good. (**disappoint**) _is disappointing_

1 We've been filming all day and we are very tired. _____ (**exhaust**)
2 I couldn't believe it when I saw a famous actor downtown. _____ (**amaze**)
3 This scene isn't interesting. We need the writer to add something funny. It _____ (**bore**)
4 *The Simpsons* is an animated sitcom. I think it's funny. _____ (**amuse**)
5 Nature documentaries interest us. We really like them. _____ (**interest**)
6 I feel sad when I listen to the news because of all the problems in the world. _____ (**depress**)

6 Complete the sentences with the correct *-ed* or *-ing* form of the words below.

| convince • embarrass • intrigue • shock • terrify • tire • ~~worry~~ |

I thought the news story about global warming was really _worrying_.

1 We were _____ and upset when we heard the news about Ferdi's accident.
2 The actor looked a lot like the man he portrayed. He was very _____.
3 I fell down in the street in front of all my friends. I was so _____!
4 The plot of that new show was very _____. I can't wait to watch it again next week.
5 What's the most _____ horror movie you've ever seen?
6 By the time Joe had completed the marathon, he was very _____.

have / get something done

7 Put the words in order to make sentences with *have* or *get something done*.

every / teeth / six / our / we / checked / have / months
We have our teeth checked every six months.

1 my / clothes / has / her / made / aunt
_____

2 house / week / decorated / our / last / got / we
_____

3 were / make-up / their / actors / having / the / done
_____

4 times / had / TV set / three / I've / this / repaired
_____

5 her / taken / she / photo / has / get / to
_____

6 you / recently / cut / have / your / had / hair ?
_____

8 Complete the sentences with the correct past participle below.

| cut • delivered • ~~done~~ • replaced • taken • written |

She got her make up _done_ by a professional make up artist. She looked amazing!

1 Have you ever had your photo _____ by a professional photographer?
2 He's had his hair _____ really short. I didn't recognize him!
3 We had our old windows _____ with new ones. They look great!
4 I ordered a new sofa online and I got it _____. It was so easy.
5 The producer decided to have two extra scenes _____ for the show.

Language reference page 75

Grammar

The passive (1)

1 Complete the sentences. Use the correct past participle of the verbs in parentheses.

1. The contestants were _____ on a desert island for ten days. (**leave**)
2. The first episode of the new reality TV show was _____ by millions of viewers. (**watch**)
3. A new character is being _____ for the next season. (**develop**)
4. That US sitcom is _____ all over the world. (**broadcast**)
5. The producer was _____ of making up storylines. (**accuse**)
6. We visited the TV studio while a new show was being _____. (**film**)

2 Match sentences 1–6 in exercise 1 with descriptions A–D.

A simple present passive ____
B present continuous passive ____
C simple past passive ___1___ ____ ____
D past continuous passive ____

3 Circle the correct alternatives.

1. Plasma screens **were being invented / were invented** in the 1960s.
2. The last episode of my favorite reality TV show **is shown / is being shown** tonight.
3. All the subway trains **were cancelled / were being cancelled** because of electrical problems.
4. Usually infomercials **are broadcast / are being broadcast** late at night.
5. Their rooms **were being cleaned / are cleaned** when they arrived at the hotel.
6. Who **is being invited / is invited** to Max's party?
7. There's a big film studio in my town. More than 200 people **are being employed / are employed** there.

4 Rewrite the active sentences as passive sentences and the passive sentences as active sentences.

People spend more and more time watching TV every day.
More and more time is spent watching TV every day.

1. They made the new reality TV show very cheaply.
   _____
2. All the Olympic events were shown all over the world.
   TV stations _____
3. They are presenting the MTV awards tonight.
   _____
4. They chose a famous actor to play the lead character.
   _____
5. The cast weren't paid much money for all their hard work.
   The producer _____
6. Millions of dollars are spent on TV commercials each year.
   Companies _____

TV Trends   6

5 Complete the text. Use the correct active or passive forms of the verbs in parentheses.

Our TV viewing habits _are changing_ (**change**) and, for young people today, TV (1) _____ (**become**) more and more interactive.

A new phenomenon, "chatterboxing", (2) _____ (**investigate**) by researchers. "Chatterboxing" is when people comment on a show while it (3) _____ (**broadcast**) via social networks and microblogging sites. It is now common for people to watch TV with a smart phone, tablet, or laptop close by.

During a recent American football game, 12,233 tweets per second (4) _____ (**send**) by viewers. Records (5) _____ (**make**) every day as the phenomenon spreads. Are you a chatterbox?

Passive questions

6 Write questions. Use the simple present passive or the simple past passive. Then choose the correct answers.

1 where / the first season of *Big Brother* / film
Where was the first season of Big Brother filmed?
A Brazil   **B** The Netherlands   **C** The UK   **D** The US

2 how many / TV sets / sell / in the US / before 1942
_____
A About 1,000   **B** Between 5 and 6,000   **C** 3,000   **D** Between 7 and 8,000

3 how many years / the sitcom *Friends* / show / on US TV
_____
A Three.   **B** Five.   **C** Ten.   **D** Twelve.

4 where / *Gossip Girl* / film
_____
A New York City   **B** Los Angeles   **C** Boston   **D** San Francisco

5 when / the *Globo* TV network / launch
_____
A 1939   **B** 1950   **C** 1965   **D** 1990

6 when / the first TV set / demonstrate
_____
A 1886   **B** 1906   **C** 1926   **D** 1946

1 B 2 D 3 C 4 A 5 C 6 C

Language reference page 74

7 Protecting Our Planet

Reading

| HOME | NEWS | PICTURES | ECONOMICS | WILDLIFE | OUR PLANET | COMMUNITY | CONTACT |

Power to the people

1 For many people, electricity is a luxury. More than 1.5 billion people around the world have no electricity supply, and almost half the global population has to rely on polluting and unhealthy fuels for cooking and for powering their homes. For this reason, efforts have been made to introduce reliable and affordable energy to businesses and households in the developing world.

Nicaragua

2 In the small Nicaraguan villages of Orinoco and Punta Marshall, electricity is supplied by diesel generators. Diesel generators are often used to supply power to rural communities in the developing world. Diesel is easy to obtain, and the generators are relatively cheap to set up. However they can be expensive to run, and they cause a lot of pollution.

3 In 2009, the Nicaraguan government and a sustainable energy company introduced electricity meters in the villages with impressive results. Before this, electricity bills in the villages had been high. The bills had been calculated according to the number of electrical appliances in each home. But after the electricity meters were installed, pollution and electricity bills were reduced. This was because residents were more aware of how much electricity was being consumed, and as a result, household energy use dropped. This meant that an estimated 21,921 liters of diesel could be saved annually. Costs were reduced by around $22,000 in one year, and carbon emissions were cut by almost 57 tons.

India

4 In Bihar, one of India's poorest states, around 85 percent of the population does not have access to the national electricity grid. The people who can afford electricity mostly use diesel generators. However, efforts have been made there to reduce the reliance on diesel, and increase access to electricity for everybody.

5 Recently, an energy company has set up biomass power plants to generate electricity using a clean, renewable energy source. Rice husks, the waste which remains after rice has been harvested, are transported to the biomass power plants and burned. This creates heat, which is consequently used to make electricity for generators and turbines.

6 80 small biomass power plants have now been set up across Bihar. They provide power to 32,000 rural homes which do not have access to the grid. As burning biomass fuel is cleaner than burning fossil fuels such as diesel, each power plant saves 125–150 tons of carbon emissions each year.

7 Thanks to programs like these, small changes in energy use are not only having an impact on the environment, but are also improving the lives of thousands of people in rural communities around the world.

Bihar rice husk power plant

---

1 Look at the title and the photo. What do you think the article is about?

2 Read statements A–E. According to the article, which one is true?

  A Electricity costs used to be low for people in Nicaragua.
  B Diesel generators are cheap to run.
  C Burning fossil fuel causes more pollution than burning biomass fuel.
  D Electricity is supplied by biomass fuel in India and Nicaragua.
  E Waste food products do not help in the production of electricity.

Protecting Our Planet 7

3 Read the article again. Choose the correct answers.

1 Diesel generators are …
   A a clean way to generate electricity.
   B cheap to run but produce a lot of emissions.
   C costly to run and produce a lot of emissions.
   D expensive to set up.
   E no longer used to supply electricity in Nicaragua.

2 Electricity bills in the two Nicaraguan villages used to be based on …
   A the amount of electrical appliances in each household.
   B the amount of people in each household.
   C electricity meter calculations.
   D the amount of electricity used the previous year.
   E the amount of electricity used by other villagers.

3 The installation of electricity meters led to …
   A an increase in electricity use.
   B no change in electricity use.
   C an increase in carbon emissions.
   D people buying and using more electrical appliances.
   E a reduction in electricity use.

4 In India, a technique has been developed that uses …
   A rice to provide electricity in homes.
   B agricultural waste to power generators.
   C agricultural waste to power the grid.
   D diesel to power generators.
   E coal to power generators.

5 Biomass power stations produce …
   A more heat than diesel generators.
   B more carbon emissions than diesel generators.
   C the same amount of carbon emissions as fossil fuel power plants.
   D fewer carbon emissions than fossil fuel power plants.
   E more energy than fossil fuel power plants.

6 Initiatives such as those in Nicaragua and Bihar can …
   A have a negative impact on the environment.
   B have no benefits for rural communities or the environment.
   C have benefits for rural communities and for the environment.
   D help large companies make more money.
   E help rural communities use more fossil fuels.

4 Match words 1–5 with synonyms or antonyms in the text.

1 necessity: antonym (n), (paragraph 1) _____
2 attempts: synonym (n), (paragraph 1) _____
3 urban: antonym (adj), (paragraph 2) _____
4 cold: antonym (n), (paragraph 5) _____
5 effect: synonym (n), (paragraph 7) _____

5 Read definitions 1–5. Match them with words in the text.

1 supplying a machine or vehicle with the energy that makes it work (paragraph 1) _____

2 devices that measure and record the amount of electricity, gas, water, etc. that you have used (paragraph 3) _____

3 machines that are designed to do a particular thing in the home (paragraph 3) _____

4 a building or group of buildings where electricity is produced (paragraph 5) _____

5 a crop which has been cut and gathered (paragraph 5) _____

Vocabulary

Verbs: environment

1 Unscramble the letters in parentheses to complete the sentences.

How much does it cost to _install_ solar panels? (**tslanil**)

1. I'm going to _____ trees this weekend as part of a reforestation project. (**patln**)
2. Can supermarkets _____ packaging to help the environment? (**deceru**)
3. Many developing countries _____ too much energy and this is damaging the planet. (**necuoms**)
4. Does your country _____ a lot of food? (**riptom**)
5. Will two wind turbines _____ enough energy for a whole town? (**retanege**)

2 Complete the headlines with the verbs below.

| allocate • depleted • importing • install • insulate |

1. **City council decides to _____ solar panels on all local government buildings.**
2. Local builder offers to _____ homes for free after building work is complete.
3. Government to _____ more land for sustainable development projects.
4. **Act now! Save energy before reserves are _____.**
5. Local supermarket stops _____ food in an attempt to stay local.

3 Circle the correct alternatives.

1. The **install / installation** of electricity meters has reduced fuel bills in that town.
2. The **deplete / depletion** of food supplies in rural communities is a result of the recent drought.
3. What is the most effective material for **insulating / insulation** a roof?
4. Coffee **plant / plantation** tours show visitors how the manufacturing process works.
5. Local businesses are trying to **consume / consumption** less energy to help the environment.
6. Is there a cheap and efficient way to **reduce / reduction** electricity costs for a large town?

Focus on phrasal verbs

4 Write four phrasal verbs. Use the words below.

| ~~cut~~ • ~~on~~ • to • out • phase • ~~down~~ • use • resort • up |

c_ut_ _down_ _on_

1. r_____ _____
2. u_____ _____
3. p_____ _____

5 Complete the sentences. Use the verbs in exercise 4.

1. Our car has broken down again, so we have had to _____ walking.
2. If we _____ all our energy resources, it will cause problems for future generations.
3. Do you think it's a good idea to _____ cars in city centers?
4. You must _____ the amount of sugar you eat. It's not good for you!

Protecting Our Planet 7

either ... or and neither ... nor

6 Complete the sentences with either ... or or neither ... nor.

I want to buy _either_ an electric car _or_ a new bike.

1 The city planners are going to install _____ solar panels _____ wind turbines.
2 _____ oil _____ coal is indispensable to modern living.
3 I would like the government to _____ phase out cars downtown _____ see more bike routes.
4 We don't have a backyard so we grow _____ fruit _____ vegetables.
5 Our town has _____ bike paths _____ good public transportation. It's difficult to get around.
6 We can _____ continue to pollute the environment _____ we can change our habits now.

Prefixes and suffixes

7 Complete the sentences. Use the words in parentheses and a prefix or suffix below.

-able • -ation • -ence • -er • -ic • -ish • -ive • -ment • re-

Which _builder_ did you use to do the work on your apartment? (**build**)

1 We'd like to _____ the place where we were born this vacation. (**visit**)
2 Do you think it's _____ not to try to protect the environment? (**self**)
3 We all need to do more to use _____ sources of energy. (**renew**)
4 What can we do to make a _____ to the planet for future generations? (**different**)
5 I've joined a _____ in my town called "Change for the Better". (**move**)
6 Alternative forms of energy are _____. That's probably why a lot of people don't use them. (**expense**)
7 More public _____ could help reduce congestion and cut carbon emissions in cities. (**transport**)
8 Shara is very _____. Have you seen her drawings of the local landscape? (**artist**)

8 Complete the bold words with the correct prefix or suffix. Use a dictionary to help you.

There was a _mis_**understanding** at the meeting, but we sorted it out in the end.

1 We _____**estimated** the work we had to do. It took a lot longer than we thought.
2 It is _____**possible** for humans to survive on Mars because of the danger from radiation.
3 Do you think having a tattoo is more **pain**_____ than having a piercing?
4 The scientist wasn't happy with the results of the experiment, so she decided to _____**do** it.
5 The communal garden looks very **attract**_____ at the moment with all the flowers on the fruit trees.

Grammar

The passive (2)

1 Read sentences 1–6. Are they active (*A*) or passive (*P*)?

Local people have been invited to hear about the new environment policy. _P_

1 We bought a new house last fall with solar panels. ____
2 My grandparents use their garden waste to help their plants grow. ____
3 All of the residents will be informed of energy-saving ideas at the next meeting. ____
4 People should be encouraged to use public transportation more. ____
5 Builders had completed the new eco-homes sooner than expected. ____
6 Energy bills could be reduced by switching off our TV sets and computers overnight. ____

2 Match sentences 1–5 with verb forms A–E.

1 We **may be damaging** the planet for future generations. ____
2 A community garden **had been discussed** at the meeting. ____
3 A new bio fuel car **will be revealed** at the car show. ____
4 Fossil fuels **have been used** for centuries. ____
5 The damage to the environment **can't be reversed**. ____

A *present perfect passive*
B *can* modal passive
C *will* future passive
D *past perfect passive*
E *may* modal passive

3 Circle the correct alternatives in the news article.

HOME | NEWS | LOCAL NEWS

April 21st (last updated 10 mins ago)

The local government (**has agreed**) / **has been agreed** to build a new eco-town and building contractors (1) **have found** / **have been found** for the project. Work will start in a few months. The project (2) **will be created** / **will create** hundreds of jobs which (3) **will benefit** / **will be benefitted** the local community. However, some local farmers are unhappy because they (4) **had told** / **had been told** the project would not affect them. The main transportation route for contractors (5) **might be set up** / **might set up** through local farming land. Farmers (6) **will be invited** / **will invite** to a meeting next week with planners to discuss the issue.

4 Complete the sentences. Use the correct form of the **bold** verbs and the information in parentheses.

Customers _have been encouraged_ (**encourage**) to reuse shopping bags. (*present perfect passive*)

1 Residents _____ (**advise**) to try to find new ways to save energy. (*past perfect passive*)
2 The new eco-friendly leisure complex _____ (**not finish**) by the end of the year. (*will future passive*)
3 Imported food _____ (**sell**) in our supermarkets for years. (*present perfect passive*)
4 Residents _____ (**tell**) about the plans to install wind turbines. (*past perfect passive*)
5 Further damage to the environment _____ (**prevent**) before it is too late. (*must* modal passive)
6 Installation of solar panels _____ (**not pay**) for by local people. (*should* modal passive)

128

Protecting Our Planet 7

5 Rewrite the active sentences as passive sentences. Omit *by* + agent where appropriate.

Climate change will affect the polar ice caps and the lives of animals.
The polar ice caps and the lives of animals will be affected by climate change.

1 I will design a website for the energy campaign next week.

2 Increased levels of air pollution could cause health problems.

3 The building company has delivered all of the materials.

4 We sell locally-sourced produce here.

5 Last month more than 1,000 people had viewed our new website.

6 A local farmer has offered us work.

6 Rewrite the active questions as passive questions. Omit *by* + agent where appropriate.

When will they install the new solar panels?
When will the new solar panels be installed?

1 Can pollution affect sea creatures?

2 Where should the energy company put the wind turbines?

3 When can we expect the results of the survey?

4 Will campaigners win the battle over the land?

5 Has your school set up an environment group?

6 How can local people reduce energy costs?

7 Circle the correct alternatives to complete the text about climate change.

The process of climate change (**1**) **has been observed / has observed** by scientists all over the world. It (**2**) **affects / is affected** different species in different ways, and it (**3**) **could be contributed / could contribute** to the extinction of certain animals and plants. Let's look at some examples.

- The Emperor penguin feeds under sea ice, but because global warming is melting the ice, the penguins (**4**) **will face / will be faced** food shortages in the near future.
- Oxygen supplies for salmon (**5**) **could be depleted / could deplete** in rivers because of an increase in water temperatures.
- The melting ice caps mean that boats can travel more easily into the waters inhabited by the Beluga whale. The whales' survival (**6**) **has threatened / has been threatened** by the increased number of people traveling in the waters.
- Koala bears (**7**) **have suffered / have been suffered** food shortages due to global warming. Koalas like to eat the leaves of the eucalyptus trees, but an increase in temperatures (**8**) **has led / has been led** to more forest fires and the destruction of trees.

Language reference page 76

8 Bad Behavior

Reading

Peculiar punishments

1. Michael Cicconetti, a judge in Ohio, US, has earned himself a reputation for being tough thanks to the unique punishments he gives to offenders. Judge Cicconetti often uses what he calls "creative justice" to make offenders confront the reality of their crimes and feel empathy for their victims.

2. On one occasion, Judge Cicconetti ordered a woman to spend a night alone in remote woods without food, shelter, a blanket, or a cell phone. She had been arrested for abandoning 35 kittens in parks. When the kittens were found, many were ill, and nine later died. Judge Cicconetti said that he wanted to make an example of the woman so as to make other people think twice before committing a similar crime. He gave her a choice of two punishments: go to prison for 90 days, or serve a reduced sentence and spend one night alone in the woods. When she chose the second option, he informed her that she was going to suffer in the same way that she had made the kittens suffer. After spending a lonely night in the woods, she served a 14-day sentence and paid $3,200 to the animal charity which had taken care of the surviving kittens.

3. The judge also punished a man who stole a charity donation box for the homeless. Again, he offered the offender a choice: a 90-day prison sentence, or one night living as a homeless person and then three days in prison. The man agreed to spend the night on the streets, and the judge ordered him to begin his 24 hours of homelessness immediately. The man left the courtroom wearing a GPS device to monitor his position, and carrying no money or personal possessions. The offender said that he understood the judge's point of view. He admitted that he shouldn't have stolen the money and was willing to accept the consequences.

4. Creative justice seems to be effective and does have an impact. An attorney who has worked with Judge Cicconetti says that it really works. "He offers offenders a choice, and hopes that they will accept his alternative punishment. So far, there have only been two people who went on to reoffend, after receiving one of his alternative punishments."

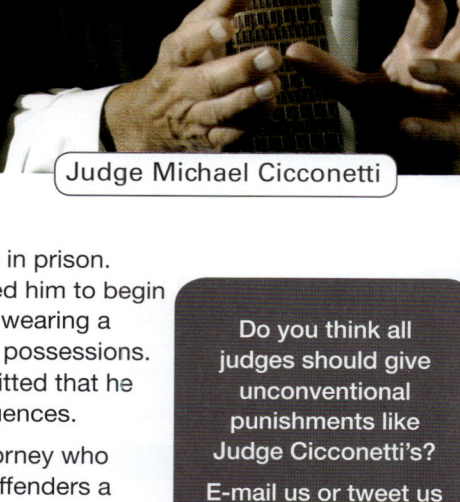

Judge Michael Cicconetti

Do you think all judges should give unconventional punishments like Judge Cicconetti's?

E-mail us or tweet us now with your views.

---

1 Look at the photos. What do you think the article is about? Skim the article and check.

2 Match definitions 1–5 with words or phrases in the article.
   1 the opinion people have about what someone is like (paragraph 1) _____
   2 not like anything else (paragraph 1) _____
   3 people who are convicted of a crime (paragraph 1) _____
   4 a cover often made from wool to keep you warm (paragraph 2) _____
   5 very unusual or different, not typical (paragraph 4) _____

Bad Behavior

3 Read the article again. Choose the correct answers.

1. Judge Cicconetti wants offenders to …
   A be given tough punishments.
   B feel embarrassed about their crimes.
   C go to prison for their crimes.
   D understand how their victims feel.
   E find alternative ways stop committing crimes.

2. The judge sentenced the woman to spend …
   A a day working at an animal charity.
   B a night with the kittens in a park.
   C a night on her own in the woods.
   D a night in prison.
   E a night looking after animals.

3. The judge wanted the woman to …
   A know what it was like to spend a night alone.
   B understand how the kittens had felt when she abandoned them.
   C understand how cats live.
   D take care of the surviving kittens.
   E be as comfortable as possible in the park.

4. The woman who abandoned the kittens …
   A also spent 14 days in prison.
   B didn't spend any time in prison.
   C also had to pay the judge $3,200.
   D also spent three days in prison.
   E also spent 90 days in prison.

5. The man who stole money for the homeless …
   A refused to accept the consequences of his actions.
   B chose to spend 90 days in prison.
   C said that he had done nothing wrong.
   D spent three nights living on the streets.
   E admitted that what he had done was wrong.

4 Read the article again. What is the main idea?

A Creative justice never works and is not an appropriate way to deal with any crime.
B Creative justice can work if the offender is prepared to accept the alternative punishment.
C Prison is the only option for anyone who has committed a crime.
D Creative justice only works with petty crimes.
E Creative justice only works because of Judge Cicconetti's personality.

5 Find words 1–5 in the article. What do they mean in context? Choose the correct definitions.

1. tough (line 2)
   A difficult
   B strict or firm

2. remote (line 7)
   A far away from places where other people live
   B not very friendly or interested in other people

3. shelter (line 7)
   A protection from rain, danger, or attack
   B the fact of having a place to live or stay, considered as a basic human need

4. abandoning (line 8)
   A leaving someone or something you are responsible for, with no intention of returning
   B stopping doing something before it is finished

5. impact (line 28)
   A an effect
   B the force of hitting one object with another

6 Look at the cartoon. What do you think the criminal did?

A He painted his house the wrong color.
B He was caught writing graffiti.
C He went to the wrong hairdressers.
D He stole some paint.
E He joined a gang.

Vocabulary

Verbs: crime and criminals

1 Complete the chart.

Verb	Noun
arrest	arrest
convict	1 _____
2 _____	supervision
offend	3 _____
incarcerate	4 _____
5 _____	punishment
sentence	6 _____
7 _____	rehabilitation
serve	8 _____

2 Complete the sentences with the verb or noun form of the words in exercise 1.
1. Parents need to _____ children in the recreational area.
2. A new therapy has been proven to _____ young offenders and prevent them from reoffending.
3. Juveniles who _____ prison sentences do not always reoffend.
4. The criminal committed the _____ during the night.
5. The judge said that the _____ fitted the crime.
6. Judges make important decisions and decide whether to _____ people of crimes.
7. Some prisoners learn new skills during their _____.
8. He was given a three-month _____ in prison and ordered to pay a large fine.
9. Police say they have made an _____ in connection with the recent burglary.

Focus on phrasal verbs

3 Complete the verbs 1–4 with particles A–D.

A off   B up   C into   D in with

1 bump _____   3 lock _____
2 cut yourself _____   4 fall _____

4 Complete the dialogues. Use the correct form of the verbs in exercise 3.
1. A Have you seen Jack recently?
   B Yes. I _____ him in the mall on the weekend.
2. A I can't believe what Rianne told me about her relatives.
   B Yes, I know. They _____ themselves _____ from the rest of the family. It's very sad.
3. A Are you leaving your bike like that?
   B No. I'm going to _____ it _____ so no one steals it.
4. A I spoke to Santi's mom the other day. She's really worried.
   B Why?
   A Well, Santi _____ some older boys and he's been very difficult at home and school recently.

Bad Behavior 8

Reporting verbs

5 Match sentences 1–5 with the different uses A–D.

A verb + (that)
B verb + object + infinitive
C verb + to + infinitive
D verb + for + gerund

The criminal agreed to apologize to the victim. _C_

1 The judge ordered the criminal to serve a three-year prison sentence. ____
2 The student apologized for behaving so badly in class. ____
3 The therapist explained that her work had a high success rate. ____
4 The thief admitted that he had stolen money and jewelry. ____
5 We all agreed to go to the internet café after school. ____

6 Choose the correct reporting verbs to complete the sentences.

1 The teenagers ____ for wasting police time.
  A apologized   B told
2 The gang ____ that they had tried to steal a car.
  A offered   B admitted
3 The therapist ____ all of her clients to do a behavior therapy course.
  A advised   B replied
4 My neighbors ____ that there had been a robbery nearby.
  A said   B told
5 The girls ____ to work together on the project.
  A announced   B agreed
6 The woman ____ to see a lawyer.
  A replied   B asked

Expressions of time and place

7 Match the direct speech time expressions 1–8 with the reported speech time expressions A–H.

1 yesterday   _E_   A the next day
2 next week   ___   B there
3 tomorrow   ___   C that day
4 now   ___   D the previous night
5 today   ___   E the day before
6 this / these   ___   F that / those
7 last night   ___   G then
8 here   ___   H the following week

8 Complete the reported sentences with the correct time and place expressions.

"My bike was stolen **today**," said Mike.
Mike said his bike had been stolen _that day_____.

1 "Someone broke into my yard **last night**," said the man.
  The man said someone had broken into his yard _____.
2 "I want to visit him in prison **tomorrow**," said the attorney.
  The attorney said he wanted to visit him in prison _____.
3 "We hope to have the latest crime statistics by **next week**," said the police officer.
  The police officer said that they hoped to have the latest crime statistics by _____.
4 "There was a big robbery **here** in 2012," the security guard said.
  The security guard said there had been a big robbery _____ in 2012.
5 "I had a meeting with the family **yesterday**," said the therapist.
  The therapist said that she had had a meeting with the family _____.
6 "I want to deal with the behavior issues **now**," explained the teacher.
  The teacher said he wanted to deal with the behavior issues _____.

Language reference page 79   133

Grammar

Reported speech

1 Match the direct speech sentences 1–5 with reported speech sentences A–D. Use one reported speech sentence twice.

1 "The judge sentences a lot of people for crimes." ___
2 "The judge sentenced a lot of people for crimes." ___
3 "The judge has sentenced a lot of people for crimes." ___
4 "The judge is going to sentence a lot of people for crimes." ___
5 "The judge will sentence a lot of people for crimes." ___

The journalist said that …

A the judge had sentenced a lot of people for crimes.
B the judge would sentence a lot of people for crimes.
C the judge was going to sentence a lot of people for crimes.
D the judge sentenced a lot of people for crimes.

2 Complete the chart with the verb forms below.

can • past perfect • present continuous • present perfect • simple past • would

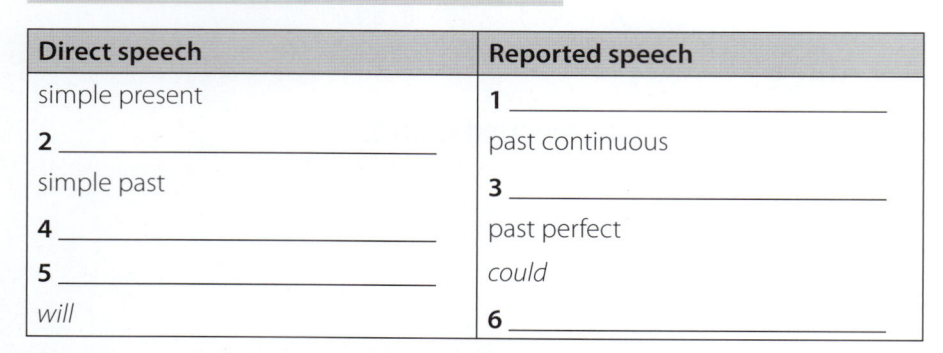

Direct speech	Reported speech
simple present	1 _____
2 _____	past continuous
simple past	3 _____
4 _____	past perfect
5 _____	could
will	6 _____

3 Rewrite the sentences in reported speech. Change the time expressions.

"I'm doing some work in the community next week," he said.
He said _he was doing some work in the community the following week_____.

1 "The judge sentenced the gang last week," she said
   She said _____.
2 "We're going to see a therapist next weekend," Devon's mother said.
   Devon's mother said _____.
3 "We'll watch *Judge Judy* on TV tonight," they said.
   They said _____.
4 "I'm not doing anything just now," Tino said.
   Tino said _____.
5 "The trial will probably finish tomorrow," the TV reporter said.
   The TV reporter said _____.
6 "I spent time in prison last year," Julio said.
   Julio said _____.

Bad Behavior 8

4 Circle the correct alternatives.

"Where did you go?" they asked her.
They asked her where she **had been** / has been.

1 "What time did you arrive at the crime scene?" the detective asked me.
The detective asked **me / I** what time **I / me** had arrived at the crime scene.
2 "When will you get home?" my dad asked me.
My dad asked me when I **would get / will get** home.
3 "Have you seen this man before?" the judge asked Adela.
The judge asked Adela if she **had seen / has seen** that man before.
4 "Did you hear the result of the trial on the internet?" I asked Roberto.
I asked Roberto if **he / him** had heard the result of the trial on the internet.

5 Rewrite the questions as reported questions.

"Are you listening to me?" the female judge asked Mario.
The female judge asked _Mario if he was listening to her_____.

1 "How are you, Karl?" asked the psychologist.
The psychologist asked Karl _____.
2 "Why weren't you at school today?" the teacher asked the girl.
The teacher asked the girl _____.
3 "Where can I contact your parents?" the police officer asked the boys.
The police officer _____.
4 "Have you ever behaved like this before, Junior?" asked the therapist.
_____.
5 "Why were you hanging out at the mall with a group of boys?" Julia's mom asked her.
_____.

6 Complete the reported orders.

"Don't walk home through the park alone," her parents said.
Her parents told her _not to walk home through the park alone_____.

1 "Stop playing on the computer," Jodi told her brother.
Jodi told her brother _____.
2 "Don't worry about coming on Saturday," Henri told me.
Henri told me _____.
3 "Run faster," the sports teacher told the class.
The sports teacher _____.
4 "Leave the court room," the judge told the jury.
The judge _____.
5 "Don't be so rude," she told them.
She _____.
6 "Listen carefully," the principal told the students.
The principal _____.

7 Choose the correct answers.

1 The police officer suggested that we ____ to a counselor.
 A talk   B talking
2 The students suggested ____ the teacher.
 A to tell   B telling
3 Leona suggested ____ a chat with them.
 A having   B to have
4 The judge suggested that they ____ behavior therapy.
 A try   B trying
5 Katia suggested ____ to the mall on the weekend.
 A to go   B going
6 Jon suggested that they ____ to school.
 A walking   B walk

Language reference page 78